Bloodline of Trauma

WRITTEN BY
BRENNAN JACQUES

This is a work of nonfiction. Some names and identifying details have been changed to protect the privacy of individuals. Any resemblance to actual persons, living or deceased, or actual events is purely coincidental, except where noted by the author.

For permissions or inquiries, contact:
Brennan Jacques
Email: [jacquespublishing23@gmail.com]

First Edition — 2025

Printed in the United States of America

ISBN: 979-8-9948163-1-8 (Hardcopy)

979-8-9948163-0-1 (Paperback)

Cover Design by [Brennan Jacques Jr]
Interior Layout by [Bre'anna Jacques]

Table of Contents

◆ ◆ ◆

Dedication

To every child who ever slept with fear as a blanket and still woke up ready to fight another day.
To the mothers who held their sons a little tighter, praying the streets wouldn't take them.
To the brothers and sisters who didn't make it out — your names are forever written in my spirit.
To my daughter, whose birth gave my life meaning when I thought it was over — you are my reason, my redemption, and my peace.
And to the city of **New Orleans**, the soil that broke me and built me back stronger — this book is not just about me.
It's about us.
It's about every survivor who turned pain into power and decided that the bloodline of trauma would end right here.

Introduction

There are two types of people in this world: those who inherit trauma, and those who transform it.
For most of my life, I didn't think transformation was possible. I thought pain was permanent — that survival was my destiny. I grew up where dreams didn't live long. Where the sound of gunfire was background noise, and hunger felt normal.

Eight kids. Two bedrooms. No peace. No plan.
We learned early that struggle doesn't wait for you to grow up — it forces you to.

This book isn't about perfection or pity. It's about process — the long, messy, heartbreaking, and beautiful process of becoming something more than what the world said you could be. It's about the boy who used to fake sickness just to have a place to sleep, the teenager who thought the streets were his only home, and the man who learned that healing can start even in the darkest cell.

When I wrote *Bloodline of Trauma*, I didn't write it for fame. I wrote it for the kids still out there trying to find themselves in chaos. For the single mothers praying their sons make it home. For the teachers who see potential hiding behind pain.

Because what I've learned is this:
You can survive anything, but survival isn't the goal — *freedom* is.
Freedom from your past, from guilt, from the cycle that raised you.

Every page of this book carries a piece of that freedom — mine, and hopefully, yours.

So before you begin, take a deep breath.
What you're about to read isn't just my story.
It's a mirror for anyone who's ever felt trapped by circumstance and still dared to dream.

We are more than our wounds. We are the proof that broken things can still build beautiful lives.

Chapter 1 — The Youngest of Six

"Trauma doesn't come overnight sometimes its in the Bloodline and you're born with it"

The first sound I remember wasn't laughter.
It was sirens.

They cut through the New Orleans air like the city's own heartbeat – fast, loud, restless. Some nights they'd fade into the distance, swallowed by the noise of traffic and shouts from the street. Other nights they stopped too close, red and blue lights painting our living room walls through the thin curtains. That's when Mama would pull us closer, whispering for us to stay quiet, her hands trembling but steady enough to make us feel safe.

I was the youngest of six children.

In a house full of noise, personalities, and survival instincts, being the youngest meant you learned early how to observe. I wasn't the strongest. I wasn't the loudest. I wasn't the one people expected to lead.

I was the one who watched.

Three of us grew up one way.
Three of them grew up another.

And the difference between those two childhoods would shape everything that followed.

We stayed in the St. Thomas Housing Development. Red brick buildings. Iron railings. Concrete courtyards where voices bounced off walls and carried through the air. The stairwells always smelled like heat, dust, and whatever somebody cooked that night.

That was my world.

But Anthony, Alfred, and Jynika — the oldest three — didn't start there with us.

They grew up downtown.

In the 7th Ward.
In the 9th Ward.

They were raised by different family members because our mom, in her younger years, wasn't stable yet. She was still trying to survive herself. Still trying to grow up while raising children. So the oldest three experienced life separated from us — moving between relatives, adapting to new rules, adjusting to new environments.

By the time the youngest three came along, life looked different.

Not fixed.

Just consolidated.

We were together under one roof in St. Thomas. And together in the projects means you experience everything as a unit — the good days, the bad days, and the unpredictable nights.

Two Childhoods in One Bloodline

The oldest three learned independence early.

They knew what it meant to live without their mother present every day. They understood displacement. They knew what it felt like to belong to a family but not always be inside the same house.

That kind of childhood hardens you differently.

By the time they were back around us consistently, they carried a downtown toughness. A sharper edge. They had seen more. Lived more. Adjusted more.

We, the youngest three, were raised together in St. Thomas — but our childhood was shaped by proximity to the streets and the weight of what had already happened before we were old enough to understand it.

Anthony, especially, felt larger than life to me.

When you're the baby, your older siblings look invincible. Anthony had presence. The way he walked. The way people acknowledged him. The way he carried himself in a crowd. He wasn't just my brother — he was someone I watched closely, even when I didn't realize I was studying him.

I didn't know then how fragile presence really is.

1993 — The Dice Game

It was 1993.

Anthony was at the St. Bernard Housing Development.

The courtyard was alive that day.

Dice games were more than gambling. They were competition. Pride. Reputation. Men circled up with folded cash in their fists. Shoes scraped concrete. Somebody always kept watch.

I picture the scene slow.

Anthony steps into the circle.

The dice hit the pavement — sharp crack against concrete.

"Ah let's eat!"

Laughter. More money hits the pile. He throws again.

The dice bounce, spin, settle.

He wins. "Pick up", "nobody moves but me"

The energy changes.

Winning is fine — until you win too much.

Smiles start tightening. The jokes stop landing the same. A couple of guys lean in closer, whispering. Somebody mutters under their breath.

Anthony collects his money.

Another throw.

Another win.

Now the air feels heavy.

In places like that, pride weighs more than cash. And pride bruises fast.

A voice raises.
"You lucky."
Another voice: "Shoot again."

Anthony doesn't back down.

It was just a game.

But in certain environments, nothing is ever just a game.

They got mad.

Not because he cheated.

Not because he disrespected anyone.

Because he won.

The shift probably happened fast — the way these things always do. A hand reaches. Someone tries to snatch. Words turn sharp. A push. A shove.

Then a moment.

A decision.

And over a dice game — over money that would've been gone by the weekend — my brother's life ended.

The Day the House Changed

I was too young to understand what death really meant.

I didn't grasp permanence.

I just knew something felt different.

Adults moved differently. Conversations dropped into whispers when we walked into rooms. The house felt heavier — like the air itself carried weight.

I remember faces more than words.

Tight jaws. Red eyes. Silence that stretched too long.

As a child, you don't say, "I'm grieving."

You don't say, "I am traumatized."

You just absorb.

Trauma doesn't always arrive loud. Sometimes it seeps in slowly — through tone, through tension, through watching your mother try to stay strong when her world just cracked open.

I didn't cry the way I probably should have. I don't even know if I fully understood that he wasn't coming back.

I just knew something was missing.

And when something leaves abruptly like that, it leaves a vacuum.

Trauma in the Bloodstream

Looking back, I understand something I couldn't name then:

Trauma was building in my bloodstream.

Not just mine — all of ours.

It lived in the way arguments felt more dangerous.
In the way protection turned into hyper-vigilance.
In the way conflict felt like it could escalate at any second.

My nervous system was learning lessons my mind was too young to comprehend.

Every loud voice made my heart jump.
Every group of men arguing made my stomach tighten.
Every dice game I saw after that carried a different meaning.

When you grow up in environments where violence can interrupt joy at any moment, your body stays alert — even during peace.

And that alertness becomes normal.

The Oldest Three vs. The Youngest Three

The oldest three experienced instability through separation — being sent to live with relatives, adjusting to different households, navigating childhood without consistent parental stability.

Their trauma was displacement.

Ours was aftermath.

We, the youngest three, grew up in the shadow of Anthony's death. We grew up watching the ripple effects.

Grief changed the temperature of the house.

Security became fragile.

Conversations about the streets carried more warning.

And I, the baby, absorbed it all without fully understanding it.

Two different childhoods.
Same bloodline.
Different scars.

Before I Knew the Word

Nobody sat us down for therapy.

Nobody explained grief counseling.

In the projects, survival is the priority.

You keep moving. You don't stop to unpack pain. You adapt.

But unprocessed trauma doesn't disappear. It embeds. It becomes reaction. It becomes temperament. It becomes instinct.

Before I ever learned the word "trauma," my body already knew it.

It was in my shoulders staying tense.
In my eyes scanning rooms.
In the way I evaluated energy before trusting it.

Anthony's death wasn't just a tragic event.

It was the first fracture in my understanding of safety.

And fractures, if ignored, widen over time.

At night, the air changed. The laughter from the kids faded, replaced by tension that even the dark couldn't hide. The streets came alive with their own language — one of whispers, footsteps, and the occasional gunshot that made everyone freeze for a heartbeat. The neighborhood was alive, but it was also haunted — by poverty, by fear, by history.

Mama did her best to keep us away from the worst of it. But how do you protect kids from the air they breathe?

I didn't understand it then, but she was teaching us resilience long before I could understand.
She taught us that survival wasn't luck — it was work. It was sacrifice. It was loving your kids so fiercely that you'd rather skip meals than watch them go hungry.

Losing a child does something to a mother that language struggles to describe.

Anthony was her first son.

Her first experience raising a boy.
Her first proof that she could bring life into this world.

And in 1993, that life was taken over a dice game.

After he died, my mother wasn't the same.

She was heartbroken — but it wasn't loud heartbreak. It wasn't dramatic scenes or constant tears. It was quiet. It was internal. It was the kind of grief that settles behind the eyes and never fully leaves.

There were days she barely communicated.

Not because she didn't love us.

But because she was carrying something too heavy to speak through.

Sometimes she would sit still for long periods, staring but not looking at anything. Conversations became shorter. Her tone softer. There were moments when it felt like she was physically present but emotionally somewhere else — maybe replaying memories, maybe asking herself what she could have done differently.

Grief rearranges a person.

It drains energy.
It reshapes priorities.
It changes how you attach.

And as children, we felt it even if we didn't understand it.

The house became quieter in a different way. Not peaceful — just fragile.

I didn't know how to comfort her. I didn't even fully understand what she was going through. I just knew my mother, the center of our world, was hurting in a way that didn't have a quick fix.

And what I know now — what makes it heavier — is that this wouldn't be the last child she would lose.

At the time, we thought the worst had already happened.

We didn't know grief would revisit our bloodline again.

What It Did to Me

Watching your mother grieve teaches you things.

It teaches you how pain can silence a person.

It teaches you that strength isn't always loud — sometimes it's just surviving another day.

But it also plants something in a young boy's spirit.

A fear of loss.
A fear of sudden endings.
A fear that happiness can be interrupted without warning.

I didn't understand death, but I understood absence.

I understood that someone who once filled space was now only a memory.

And without realizing it, I started bracing myself for life.

That's what trauma does when it enters early.

It teaches you to brace.

I Guess Life Continues

Anthony's death was the first wound I didn't know I was carrying. It was the beginning of a pattern I couldn't yet see — loss threading itself through our family like an inheritance. Before I ever knew the word trauma, it was already moving through us, passed down in silence, in grief, in survival. I was the youngest of six, born into two different childhoods and one shared pain. And what I didn't understand then was that this was only the beginning of the bloodline I would one day have to confront.

Chapter 2 — Now It Was Five

When the Hospital Became Home

There was a time when we didn't have anywhere to go.

After my brother Anthony was killed, everything fell apart. The grief alone was heavy — but grief doesn't pause rent. It doesn't stop eviction notices. It doesn't protect you from being put out of your apartment.

We were hurting and homeless at the same time.

That's a different kind of trauma.

When we got put out, there wasn't a backup plan waiting. No relative with extra space. No emergency fund. Just us — trying to survive the day while still trying to process losing Anthony.

Nights were the hardest.

Because when the sun goes down and you don't have a place to lay your head, reality hits different. The streets feel colder. The world feels smaller. Pride doesn't matter anymore. Only survival does.

And survival makes you creative.

We started faking sickness just to have somewhere to sleep at night.

We would go to the hospital and complain about stomach pains. Headaches. Chest tightness. Anything that would get us admitted long enough to stay overnight. We learned how to sound convincing. Learned how to describe symptoms just right. Learned how to act tired enough, hurt enough.

The hospital became shelter.

Those hospital beds became temporary homes.

Monitors beeping in the background. Nurses walking in and out. The smell of antiseptic in the air. That became normal for us. Not because we were sick — but because we were displaced.

Think about that.

Kids pretending to be sick just to feel safe for a night.

That does something to you.

It teaches you early that stability isn't promised. That safety is temporary. That you have to find ways to survive even if it means bending the truth. It plants a seed in your mind that says, *"The system isn't built for you — so you better figure it out."*

We weren't criminals in that moment.

We were grieving.
We were homeless.
We were scared.

But trauma doesn't announce itself politely. It builds quietly. Layer by layer. Night by night.

And when people ask me how I understand the survival mindset of these kids today, I think back to those hospital nights.

Back to pretending to be sick just to have a bed.

Back to losing Anthony and losing our home at the same time.

That's when survival mode first became normal for us.

And once survival becomes normal, it's hard to switch it off.

New Environment

Al — Alfred.
Nika — Jynika and her 2 kids.(Mae and Bill) My niece and my nephew.
Lonk — Rivers.
Baybay — Nyron.
And me, Brennan.

Anthony was gone.

You don't realize how much space one person takes up until they're not there anymore. Even in a crowded house, the absence echoed.

My niece and my nephew would cover for the empty space that my brother left absent.

Not to mention but me and my niece Mae was the exact same age, actually she is 6 days older than me. My mom and my sister was pregnant at the same time, then boom me and Mae is six days apart. How ironic. Im pretty sure you could tell we grew up to be the best of friends.

Among the youngest three, Lonk was the oldest. Then Baybay. Then me — still the baby of the babies. We moved through life in a pack. If one fought, we all fought. If one ran, we all ran. If one was hurting, none of us said it — but we felt it.

The St. Thomas Housing Development wasn't just where we stayed anymore.

It was home. And home didn't mean safe.

Learning the Environment

Growing up in St. Thomas meant you earned your place.

You learned who to speak to. Who not to look at too long.
Which buildings had tension. Which corners stayed active.

We got our fair share of fights early. Not because we were looking for trouble — but because in the projects, trouble doesn't need an invitation.

Sometimes it was about respect.
Sometimes it was about territory.
Sometimes it was about nothing at all.

We were grieving, but nobody would've known it from the outside. Grief in our environment didn't look like tears — it looked like guarded energy. When we met new people, there was tension. We didn't trust easy. We didn't laugh too loud around strangers. We sized people up before shaking hands.

We had already learned that life can flip over something small.

A dice game.
A disagreement.
A bruised ego.

Still, this was where we made our first real friends.

Boys who lived two buildings down.
Kids we ran ball with on cracked courts.
Friends who understood our silence because they carried their own.

We played sports in between sirens.
We joked in between arguments.
We learned loyalty in between chaos.

But no matter how much laughter we found, violence always hovered nearby.

Gunshots weren't rare.
Dice games were constant.
Arguments escalated quick.

It wasn't dramatic — it was normal.

That's what makes it dangerous.

One Year Later — Another Call

About a year after we were back living in St. Thomas, the phone rang.

It was one of those calls that shifts the room before you even know the details.

A family member was on the other end.

Al was getting arrested.

At first, it didn't even register. Arrested? For what?

Then we learned the charge.

Attempted murder.

They said he shot someone in the head.

I remember the air going still again — just like when Anthony died. Different situation. Same heaviness.

Al wasn't dead.

But he was gone.

He would spend the next thirteen years in prison.

Thirteen years.

When you're a kid, thirteen years sounds like forever. It sounds like another lifetime. It sounds like someone disappearing into a system you don't fully understand.

And just like that, we weren't five anymore.

We were four in the free world.

Eight in a Two-Bedroom

Not to mention, Nika had two kids by then.

So technically, it was eight of us in that two-bedroom apartment in the projects.

Eight bodies.
Two bedrooms.
One small kitchen.
One bathroom.

Space was tight. Privacy didn't exist. Somebody was always awake. Somebody was always moving. Somebody was always needing something.

Mattresses on floors.
Shared closets.
Shared air.

And outside those walls was St. Thomas — still loud, still unpredictable, still shaping us whether we wanted it to or not.

Watching Mom Break Again

My mom was still grieving Anthony.

That grief hadn't healed. It had just settled.

And now, she had to process another loss — this time, not death, but incarceration.

She wasn't just mourning a son who died.

She was mourning a son who was still alive but unreachable.

Prison is a different kind of death for a mother.

You know your child is breathing — but you can't touch him when you want. You can't protect him. You can't see what he's going through. You can't fix it.

I watched my mom carry both.

The grief of Anthony.
The fear for Al.

Sometimes she seemed emotionally exhausted. Like her spirit was stretched thin. Conversations would pause in the middle. Her eyes would drift. She would get quiet again — that same quiet from 1993, but deeper now.

It wasn't dramatic.

It was heavy.

She had to be strong for the four of us still at home. She had to show up for Nika's kids. She had to survive financially. She had to function.

But I could see the weight.

Two sons gone in different ways.

One buried.
One locked away.

And we were still kids, trying to understand the system of consequences, streets, survival, and pain all at once.

What It Did to Us

Anthony's death planted fear.

Al's incarceration planted reality.

We saw how fast a decision can change your entire future. We saw how one moment — one trigger — can cost you years.

In St. Thomas, prison wasn't rare. It was almost expected. But when it's your brother, it hits different.

We started moving more carefully.

Or at least, we thought we did.

But we were still young boys in an environment that normalized risk.

We still saw the dice games.
Still heard the gunshots.
Still felt the tension.

We just carried more inside now.

More caution.
More anger.
More confusion.

And trauma kept layering itself quietly — like bricks stacking on top of each other.

Damn Damn Damn!!

First Anthony.
Then Al.

One taken by the streets.
One taken by the system.

And we were still children trying to grow up inside it all.

St. Thomas didn't pause for our pain. The world didn't slow down to give us time to process. Life kept moving, and so did we — learning too early that survival sometimes means carrying more than a child should ever have to carry.

We were only in Chapter Two of our lives.

And already, the bloodline was shifting again.

Chapter 3 — The Day Something Shifted

"Love is the only medicine that doesn't need a prescription."

St. Thomas was where we slowly began trying to find ourselves again. After losing Anthony and then watching Al disappear into the system, there was a period where everything felt unstable, like the ground beneath us could shift at any moment. But life in the projects does not stop for grief. You either sink into it, or you find something to hold onto. For us, that something became sports.

We played football in the courtyard, basketball on cracked concrete courts, anything that let us release energy that didn't have a name yet. When we were running routes or arguing about fouls, for a moment we were just kids. We weren't the brothers of someone killed. We weren't the brothers of someone incarcerated. We were just boys competing, laughing, pushing each other to be better. Sports gave us structure. It gave us rules. It gave us a scoreboard where outcomes felt fair. In a world that felt unpredictable, that mattered.

But even while we were finding an outlet, violence was quietly rising around us again. In the St. Thomas Housing Development, tension never fully disappeared. It just waited. Arguments over money, over respect, over pride were common. We had grown used to raised voices in the distance, to dice games that carried an undercurrent of risk. Still, nothing prepares you for the moment when violence happens directly in front of you.

I remember the first time I saw someone get killed.

We were playing football in the front courtyard, running routes between parked cars and light poles like we always did. The sun was still out, and the air felt ordinary. There were maybe six or seven of us out there, arguing about whether a pass was complete or not. It felt like any other day.

Then two men entered the courtyard.

At first, nobody paid them much attention. Grown men arguing wasn't unusual. One of them said he wanted his money. The other insisted he didn't have it. Their voices were sharp, but still controlled. We kept playing, pretending not to listen, though everyone heard every word.

Talking turned into yelling. Yelling turned into screaming. The kind of screaming where pride and anger mix together and logic disappears. Within seconds they were in each other's faces. Then came the pushing. The swinging. The chaos.

It escalated so fast it almost felt unreal.

And then the gunshots.

The sound cracked through the courtyard, louder than anything I had ever heard up close. Everything slowed down and sped up at the same time. My body reacted before my mind did. Me and my friends froze for half a second, completely lost, then scrambled in different directions trying to get out of sight. I remember diving behind a car, my heart pounding so hard it felt like it was in my throat. I remember the silence that followed, heavy and shocking.

Someone had been shot.

And this time, it wasn't a story we heard about later. It wasn't whispers through adults. It happened right in front of us, interrupting a game of football like it was nothing.

That night, I went home and sat in the bathtub longer than usual. I let the water run and just stared at the wall. I replayed the entire scene in my head over and over. The voices. The yelling. The first punch. The gunshots. I kept thinking about how normal the day had started and how quickly it had turned into something permanent.

I did not know then how much that moment would shape me.

I did not have the language to say I was traumatized. I just knew I felt different. Something inside me hardened that night. It was as if my mind decided that shock was too heavy to carry, so it replaced it with numbness.

After that day, I began to notice a change in myself. Things that would have scared me before did not hit the same way. Loud arguments no longer startled me as much. I started reacting faster, talking sharper. I found myself getting into more altercations in the neighborhood, almost like my body was operating in defense mode even when it didn't need to be.

A couple of days after the shooting, I got into my first real fight outside of the ones I had with my brothers. Growing up, me and Baybay fought all the time. That was different. That was brother tension. This felt different. This felt personal.

It started small, like most fights do. Words exchanged. A misunderstanding. Maybe someone testing boundaries. Normally I might have walked away, but something in me was already charged. I could feel the anger sitting just beneath the surface, and it did not take much to pull it out.

When the punches started flying, I did not hesitate. I remember the rush of adrenaline, the tunnel vision, the way everything else faded out except the person in front of me. It was not just about the argument anymore. It was like I was fighting everything I had seen and never processed.

Looking back, I understand that I was not just reacting to that one moment. I was carrying Anthony. I was carrying Al. I was carrying the image of a man falling in front of me while we were supposed to be children playing football. The fight was not just about pride. It was about survival. It was about proving I would not be caught off guard. It was about trying to feel control in a world that kept showing me how little control we really had.

St. Thomas was shaping us again. Sports gave us discipline, but violence kept teaching us lessons we were too young to fully understand. Each experience layered on top of the last. And instead of breaking down, I started building armor.

The problem with armor is that it protects you, but it also changes you.

I did not cry about what I saw. I did not talk about it. I adjusted. I became quieter in some ways, quicker in others. I thought being numb meant being strong.

I did not realize that numbness is just pain that has not found a safe place to go.

And slowly, without me even noticing, I was becoming someone who could survive chaos — but was also starting to carry it inside.

"Sometimes, survival looks like pretending you're broken."

Chapter 4 — The First Taste

The Brother Who Moved Different

By the time we were fully settled into life at the St. Thomas Housing Development, Baybay had already separated himself from the rest of us in a way that felt both impressive and dangerous. Out of the younger three—Lonk, Baybay, and me—

he was the most aggressive,

the most restless,

and the least afraid of confrontation. It felt like he had something boiling inside of him at all times. My mom would get calls from neighbors or see him walk through the door with scuffed knuckles and a look in his eyes that said he had already justified whatever happened. He fought often, and not just with kids his age. Sometimes it was older boys. Sometimes it was over respect. Sometimes it was over something so small that, from the outside, it looked pointless. But in the projects, pride and identity were currency, and Baybay refused to feel small.

From Candy to Cars

At first, his rebellion showed up in ways that seemed almost harmless. He would come home with candy stuffed in his pockets or snacks he had taken from the store. He treated it like a joke, like it was nothing more than beating the system for a few dollars' worth of sugar. We laughed about it because we were still kids, and stealing candy did not feel like it carried the weight of real consequences. But what starts small rarely stays small when there is no interruption.

The candy turned into bicycles. He began showing up riding bikes we knew he had not paid for. They were too new, too clean, too different from anything we had seen him with before. When we asked questions, he would shrug it off, sometimes smiling, sometimes brushing us away like we were thinking too hard about it. It did not take long to understand that he was testing boundaries and realizing how far he could go without getting caught.

Then one day, it was not bikes anymore. It was cars.

Stealing a car felt like something from a movie, not something happening in our own neighborhood. But Baybay had started hanging around older guys who moved differently. They did not just talk about hustling; they practiced it. They taught him which cars were easier to take—older models without advanced security systems, cars that people left unlocked, vehicles that blended in easily once you drove them off. He described to us how they would move through parking lots late at night, checking door handles quietly, listening for any alarm or sudden noise. If a door opened, that was step one. If it did not, they knew how to break in without drawing too much attention.

The Night of the Steering Column

He explained how the steering column could be forced open, exposing the wiring underneath. The first time he told me about it, he described the sound of plastic cracking and metal snapping as if it were a badge of honor. Once inside, the goal was to manipulate what needed to be manipulated until the engine turned over. When it finally did, he said it felt like conquering something. Your heart would be racing, adrenaline flooding your body, but once the car started, the fear would shift into excitement. It was not just about transportation. It was about proving you could take something that was not yours and make it move under your control.

"What begins as curiosity can quietly grow into identity."

Sometimes they kept the cars for a few hours just to ride through the city, music playing loud, windows down, feeling untouchable. Other times they stripped parts or used them in other hustles before abandoning them somewhere else. The money that came from those moves showed up in thick rolls stuffed in his pockets. He did not count it neatly at the table. He peeled it off in stacks, sometimes giving us a glimpse before reminding us not to say anything to Momma.

At first, he kept the details to himself. But eventually, he started explaining how he was getting the money, and those explanations changed something in me and Lonk. We had grown up watching loss take from our family. We had watched our mom struggle. We had seen how quickly life could strip you of control. Now here was our brother talking about taking control back, even if it was the wrong way. Money in our environment did not just represent wealth. It represented leverage. It meant you did not have to ask. It meant you did not have to wait. It meant you could move.

That sparked something in us. Curiosity became fascination. Fascination became desire. We told ourselves we were not scared. We told ourselves we were ready. In reality, we had no idea what we were stepping into. But when you grow up feeling like life keeps happening to you, the opportunity to make something happen yourself—even something illegal—can feel empowering.

The Hundred Dollar Hook

The first time I touched drugs was not planned. It happened in the same courtyard where we played football, the same space that had already seen arguments, laughter, and gunshots. We were arguing over a pass when Slim came running toward us. He moved like someone who knew he had no time to waste. Without stopping, he threw a small package toward the first person in front of him. That person was me. I caught it without thinking, purely out of instinct.

I did not even know what it was in that moment. It was wrapped tightly and small enough to disappear into my palm. Slim kept running, and seconds later police cars passed the end of the block with lights flashing. Everything happened so fast that my brain could not process it in real time. When it clicked that he had been running from the police and that I was now holding whatever he had tossed, my heart began pounding so loudly I could feel it in my ears. I slipped it into my pocket and forced myself to keep standing there like nothing had changed.

Those few minutes felt longer than they probably were. Every movement in my peripheral vision felt like a threat. I imagined officers coming back and lining us up. I imagined being searched. I imagined my mom finding out. Eventually, Slim returned, calm now, as if the urgency had never existed. He asked for it back, and when I handed it over, he looked at me with a seriousness I had not seen before. He gave me a hundred dollars and told me I had saved his life.

That hundred dollars felt unreal. I stared at it later, turning it over in my hands, thinking about how quickly it had appeared. I had not worked a job. I had not asked for it. I had simply held something for a few minutes. That was the moment something shifted inside me. It showed me how fast money could come in this world and how easy it could feel compared to everything else.

"It wasn't the money that hooked me. It was how easy it came."

Not long after, Slim handed me my own package. This time, it was not accidental. He told me it was mine to move. I remember holding it and feeling a mix of excitement and confusion. I did not fully understand the product or the process. I only understood that it represented entry into something bigger than the courtyard football games. I called my brother and told him what I had. There was a silence on the line before he began giving instructions. He explained how to move carefully, who to trust, who to avoid, and how quickly things could go wrong if I got sloppy.

His voice carried caution, but I heard opportunity. I felt older than I was. I felt important. I felt like I was no longer just watching life unfold around me but stepping into it. I did not realize that I was also stepping deeper into a cycle that had already taken so much from our family.

Looking back, I see how trauma and opportunity collided in that moment. I had grown numb to violence. I had built armor around my emotions. The streets did not scare me the way they once might have. The money made me feel alive, and that feeling overpowered everything else. I did not see chains forming. I saw independence. I did not see risk stacking up. I saw progress.

What I did not understand was that every decision was building momentum. And momentum, once it picks up speed, does not slow down just because you change your mind.

Chapter 5 — The First Escape

For the first time in my life, I found something that made the world quiet.
It wasn't church, or school, or the streets — it was a ball. Just a worn-out basketball with faded lines and too many stories in its grip.

The court behind our building was cracked and half-covered in weeds. The rim leaned sideways, the net torn, but when I stepped onto that concrete, something inside me shifted. The noise of sirens, the arguing neighbors, the hunger, the fear — all of it faded into the background. It was just me, the ball, and the rhythm of control.

Sports became my sanctuary before I even knew what that word meant.

I was around twelve when it started. My friends and I would spend hours outside, even when the sun burned hot enough to melt our shoes. We didn't have proper uniforms or coaches back then — just ambition and a ball that barely bounced.

Every layup felt like defiance. Every dribble sounded like rebellion.
Out there, I wasn't poor. I wasn't hungry. I wasn't the kid from the projects.
I was just a player.

Mama didn't understand it at first. She thought I was wasting time, running in circles, sweating for nothing. But when she saw how it kept me away from the corners, from the boys with guns and quick money, she stopped complaining. Sometimes she'd even show up to watch. She never clapped or yelled, just stood there with her arms folded, a small smile tugging at her lips. That smile was all the approval I needed.

"Freedom doesn't always look like escape. Sometimes, it's just finding something that makes you forget where you are."

Learning the Rules

The first real coach I had was a man named Mr. Temple.
He was a retired PE teacher who volunteered to work with kids from the neighborhood. He wasn't easy on us. He didn't believe in excuses, not even the ones that were true. When I told him I couldn't make practice because I had to watch my siblings, he just nodded and said, "Then bring them."

He saw something in me — hunger, discipline, focus — maybe all three.
"Basketball will teach you life," he used to say. "If you listen."

At the time, I thought he meant teamwork and drills. But what he was really teaching was endurance. He was teaching how to fail and keep going. How to fall and not let the ground claim you.

Under his watch, I ran until my legs shook, shot until my arms burned, and learned what it meant to push past pain. There were days I wanted to quit. But every time I thought about quitting, I'd remember Mama crying over bills, and suddenly quitting didn't seem like an option.

That court became my classroom, and Mr. Temple — my first real mentor.
He didn't care about where I came from. He cared about where I was going.

Finding Brotherhood

Sports gave me something the streets couldn't — brotherhood without betrayal.
On the court, we argued, fought, and cursed, but when the game started, we moved as one. There was no rich or poor, no black or white, no lost or found — just players chasing the same goal.

For the first time, I learned trust.
If I passed the ball, I knew someone would be there to catch it.
If I missed a shot, someone would rebound for me.

That kind of reliability was foreign to me. In the streets, trust could get you killed. But in the game, it was the foundation of everything.

I became good — not just decent, but *noticed*.
People started talking. Coaches came around. Local tournaments invited us. I started dreaming — small dreams at first. Maybe a scholarship. Maybe a way out.

But dreams, I would learn, can be dangerous when you come from a place that doesn't believe in them.

Between Two Worlds

As basketball pulled me one way, the streets pulled me another.
The same boys who used to shoot hoops with me started shooting guns.
They'd show up with new shoes, gold chains, money in their pockets — things I couldn't afford. I'd come home sore and sweaty from practice, and they'd come home rich.

Temptation is loud when you're broke.
And the streets are persuasive teachers.

Mr. Temple warned us. "That money don't last," he'd say. "But your freedom? That's priceless."

I wanted to believe him. But when your brother asks why there's no food, and you see other boys feeding their families off street cash, it's hard to hold faith in delayed dreams.

I tried to balance both. Practice by day, the block by night.
But you can't serve two masters forever.

The Taste of Freedom

Despite the struggle, there were moments — real moments — where I felt alive.
One summer, our team made it to the city tournament. It was the biggest event I'd ever been part of. The gym was packed, the air heavy with sweat and excitement. I remember stepping onto the court and feeling something inside me whisper, *You belong here*.

The first whistle blew, and everything went still. I played like I had nothing to lose — because I didn't. Every point, every steal, every dive was personal. It wasn't just about winning a game. It was about proving that I existed beyond my ZIP code.

When the final buzzer sounded and we won, I felt weightless.
People were cheering, coaches shaking my hand, strangers calling my name.
For one brief moment, I wasn't a statistic — I was a star.

That night, when I walked home under the streetlights, I didn't feel small. I didn't feel scared. The city didn't seem so cruel.
For the first time, I believed I could change my story.

"Sometimes, all it takes is one victory to make you forget a thousand losses."

Mama's Pride

When I walked through the door, trophy in hand, Mama was sitting at the table sorting mail. She looked up, saw me, and her whole face changed. She didn't cry, but her eyes glistened.
"I knew you had it in you," she said quietly.

That night, she cooked our favorite meal — rice, beans, and fried chicken — even though I knew she'd spent her last money on it. "You brought pride to this house," she told me.

That meant more to me than the trophy.
Because for years, all I'd brought home were problems.

That night, for the first time, I saw what hope looked like on my mother's face.

The Cracks in the Dream

But dreams are fragile things.
The same streets that raised me were jealous of my freedom.

One night after practice, I got jumped by two older guys. They weren't after money — they were after the idea of me. The kid who thought he could make it out. The one who got too much attention. They beat me until I couldn't see straight.

When I came home, Mama cried silently as she cleaned the blood from my face. She didn't ask who did it. She didn't have to.

The next morning, I still went to practice.
Mr. Temple just looked at me, eyes full of pride. "Now that's what I call heart," he said.

"Pain doesn't just break you. Sometimes, it refines you."

The Turning Point

Basketball kept me alive longer than I realized. It gave me focus when the world offered none. It gave me role models when my father wasn't there. It gave me discipline in a place built on chaos.

But the truth is, the game couldn't pay bills. It couldn't stop eviction notices. It couldn't buy groceries. And when the weight of reality got too heavy, even the strongest dreams began to bend.

I started skipping practices. Hanging out with the wrong people again. Mr. Temple saw it — he tried to pull me back. But by then, I was already sliding.

I told myself I could handle both worlds.
I was wrong.

Because the thing about escape is that it's temporary — unless you learn how to build freedom within yourself.

And back then, I wasn't building.
I was running.

"The first escape isn't the one that saves you. It's the one that shows you what saving feels like."

Chapter 6 — When the Bricks Came Down

When they started tearing down the St. Thomas Housing Development, it felt like they were tearing down more than buildings. They were tearing down memories, mistakes, fights, losses, and everything that had shaped us. The bricks that once echoed with gunshots and laughter were reduced to dust. Courtyards that had raised us were flattened like they never existed. Watching it happen felt strange. St. Thomas had been chaotic, painful, and dangerous—but it had also been ours.

With the demolition came uncertainty. We were back to scrambling, back to searching for stability. My mom was exhausted from leaning on family members whenever things fell apart. Staying with relatives had become routine, but this time she said it would be the last resort. Pride had finally outweighed convenience. She wanted something stable, even if it meant sacrificing comfort.

Searching for Stability

Finding housing was harder than we expected. My mom wasn't working, Section 8 would only cover so much, and most of the real financial weight rested on my stepfather's income. We looked at places that were too expensive, too small, or unwilling to accept our situation.

Every conversation with a landlord felt like explaining why we deserved a chance. Deposits were high. Expectations were higher.

My sister, who now had three children of her own, still managed to step up for us. She was navigating her own storms but somehow found ways to help keep ours from collapsing. She made calls, connected dots, even stole out the stores to keep a smile on our faces and stretched dollars. Eventually, she found her own place and moved forward with her kids, trying to build something steady for them. That shift left us feeling both proud and exposed.

The only real option left was the Westbank—what others called the Westbank—over in Harvey. It wasn't glamorous, but it was available. Crossing the river felt symbolic, like we were leaving one chapter behind whether we were ready or not.

"Sometimes you don't move because you're ready. You move because staying is no longer an option."

A Slower Pace, A Faster Temper

Moving to Harvey slowed the environment down. In St. Thomas, life moved at a hundred miles per hour. In Harvey, it felt like someone cut that speed in half. Streets were quieter. There was more space between houses. You could hear yourself think.

But slowing down physically doesn't mean you slow down mentally.

We carried our intensity with us.

The very first day we moved in, we got into a fight. It didn't take long for new faces to test unfamiliar ones. Words were exchanged, pride got involved, and suddenly it was me and both my brothers against three guys from the neighborhood. It was raw and immediate. We fought like we had something to defend, maybe because we did. We beat them bad enough that they called the police.

When the sirens came, we didn't flinch.

Police presence was familiar. It didn't rattle us the way it might have rattled other kids. That realization hit me later. Being unfazed by flashing lights isn't normal—it's conditioning.

"When chaos becomes routine, calm feels suspicious."

New Schools, Same Patterns

Starting at a new school meant new teachers, new hallways, new expectations. For a moment, it felt like a reset. A chance to rewrite who we were. Lonk tried at first. He showed up. He engaged. But within the first week, he was in a fight. That one fight spiraled into expulsion, and just like that, the reset disappeared.

Baybay didn't even attempt to play along. After the ninth grade, school was finished in his mind. He had tasted fast money, and once you taste that, textbooks feel slow and irrelevant. Sitting in class felt pointless when the streets were offering cash immediately. He had already decided which system he trusted more.

I was different—for a while. I still believed sports could save me. When things felt overwhelming, I ran to the court or the field. Basketball and football became therapy sessions without a therapist. The court didn't care about my family's history. The scoreboard didn't judge me. Sports gave me discipline, structure, and something to chase that wasn't illegal.

"Sports gave me rules in a life that rarely had any."

But even as I tried to anchor myself in athletics, my surroundings kept pulling at me.

Flash and Fire

It wasn't long before Lonk began stepping deeper into the drug game too. Where Baybay was reckless and loud, Lonk was smooth but flashy. If he made a thousand dollars, you would know it. He would peel bills out slowly, let them fan in his hand, make sure everyone saw what he was carrying. It wasn't subtle. It was intentional.

He liked the reaction. The nods. The quiet respect.

If he had ten hundred-dollar bills, he wanted the world to see all ten.

Watching him count money openly felt powerful and dangerous at the same time. Flashiness builds reputation, but it also builds attention. And attention, in that world, cuts both ways.

"Money talks loud in neighborhoods that feel silent."

I watched both of my brothers move deeper into that lane. One dropped out. One got expelled. Both were earning in ways that looked easier than practice drills and conditioning workouts. I would come home from training sweaty and tired, while they came home energized and counting cash.

The contrast was loud.

The Better and the Worse

Moving to Harvey did change things—for better and for worse.

For the better, there was breathing room. Fewer sirens. Fewer constant interruptions. I had more chances to focus on sports. I met new coaches. I experienced a different environment. There were moments when I could actually see a version of myself that didn't end in jail or a graveyard.

For the worse, the hustle followed us. The mindset followed us. The hunger for quick validation followed us. The demolition of St. Thomas didn't demolish what it built inside us.

The slower pace almost created space for temptation to grow stronger. Without constant chaos distracting us, the decisions we made became more intentional. There were fewer excuses. When my brothers chose the streets, it wasn't because they were surrounded by it every second —it was because they were drawn to it.

And I stood in the middle.

One foot in sports.
One foot in the influence of my brothers.

I could feel things shifting. The choices we were making now felt heavier than the fights in courtyards or the stolen bikes. These decisions felt like they had long-term consequences attached to them, even if we didn't speak it out loud.

"Every new beginning carries old habits if you don't confront them."

Crossing the River

Crossing the river to the Westbank felt like progress, but progress isn't always linear. It felt like we had slowed from one hundred miles per hour to fifty, but fifty miles per hour is still fast enough to crash.

We had a chance at something different.

We also had momentum pulling us toward something familiar.

The demolition of St. Thomas removed the physical structure of our past, but it didn't remove the mindset. And unless something shifted inside us, geography alone would never save us.

"You can leave the projects behind, but if you're not careful, the projects don't leave you."

This was the season where things began to change—for better and for worse. Opportunities started appearing. So did consequences. And for the first time, it felt like the direction of my life was no longer just about survival.

It was about choice.

And choice, I was learning, can either break a cycle—or repeat it.

Chapter 7 — On The Fence

By that time, the lines between who we were and who we were becoming were starting to blur.

Lonk graduated.

Baybay didn't.

And I was still in high school, standing in the middle of two very different futures, trying to decide which one felt more like me.

Lonk had started getting his name known in the hustle game. He wasn't loud about it in the reckless way Baybay had been. He was smooth, calculated, patient. He understood presentation. He understood relationships. He knew how to talk to people. He moved with finesse, and people respected that. His name started circulating in quiet conversations. He wasn't just another kid from across the river anymore—he was building an identity.

Baybay, on the other hand, was getting his name known in a different way. His reputation wasn't built on smooth talking or subtle plays. It was built on force. If something needed to be handled aggressively, he handled it. If somebody owed something, he pressed it. His name carried weight because people knew he didn't hesitate.

Lonk was finesse.

Baybay was aggression.

And then there was me.

I was a mix of both.

I had the hustle mentality. I understood strategy. I could read situations well. I also had the aggression when needed. But I also had something else—real thinking ability. I could see consequences before they happened. I could visualize outcomes. I could feel when something might spiral.

That's what kept me on the fence.

I didn't know if I wanted to play ball seriously and chase something structured, or follow in my brothers' footsteps and step fully into the street life that was already within arm's reach.

"When you grow up between survival and opportunity, both feel familiar."

The Energy Shift

As we got more settled in Harvey, some of our old friends started coming around more often. Guys from Uptown. Familiar faces from the old environment. They would come by the house, hang out, talk, laugh, reminisce about St. Thomas days.

But the neighborhood we were in didn't like it.

Harvey had its own identity, its own pride, its own boundaries. Outsiders weren't automatically welcomed, especially not outsiders with energy like ours. We carried ourselves with confidence, sometimes with edge. And when you mix that with territorial pride, tension doesn't take long to surface.

You could feel it building.

Looks held a little longer.
Comments got sharper.
Small exchanges carried bigger meaning.

It wasn't just about individuals anymore. It became something bigger.

Uptown vs. Harvey.

Lines were drawn without anyone officially announcing them.

"Territory isn't just land. It's pride."

The Night It Exploded

The fight didn't start huge.

It started like most conflicts do—words exchanged between a few guys. A challenge. A response. Someone stepping a little too close. Someone refusing to back down.

But this wasn't a one-on-one.

This was groups forming.

Our friends from Uptown were at our house. Guys from the neighborhood gathered quickly. Within minutes, it wasn't a conversation anymore. It was a full-blown gang fight in the middle of the neighborhood we lived in.

It was chaos.

Punches flying everywhere. Bodies colliding. People grabbing whatever they could find. I remember the sound more than anything—the thuds of fists landing, the shouting, the confusion. It wasn't organized. It wasn't controlled. It was raw emotion and territorial pride exploding at once.

Some people got hurt bad.

Broken arms. Black eyes. Faces swollen beyond recognition. Blood on shirts. People stumbling but still trying to swing.

It wasn't a movie scene. It wasn't dramatic in a glamorous way.

It was ugly.

And in the middle of it, I felt something strange.

Part of me was locked in, reacting, defending, moving instinctively. Another part of me was watching it all from a distance in my own head, thinking, "This is escalating too far."

That internal split was becoming more common for me.

"I was fighting outside, but thinking inside."

Eventually someone called the police.

Again.

Sirens cut through the noise. People scattered. Some tried to clean themselves up. Others ran. A few stood their ground until lights flashed too close to ignore.

We had already built a pattern with law enforcement in that neighborhood. So when officers arrived, they weren't just responding to a random disturbance. They were responding to a house that had already caused problems.

That changed everything.

Moving Again

It didn't take long before it became clear we had to move.

Again.

This time it wasn't demolition pushing us out. It was reputation. It was conflict. It was the reality that staying there would only mean more tension, more fights, more police presence.

Moving to another part of Harvey felt exhausting.

We had just adjusted. Just found our rhythm. And now we were packing again. Boxes. Bags. Conversations about "starting fresh" that sounded too familiar.

My mom was tired.

We were tired.

But we moved.

"Every time we tried to settle, something unsettled us."

Standing at the Crossroads

At this point, the direction of my life felt closer to decision than ever before.

Lonk was fully respected in the hustle game.

Baybay was fully feared in his lane.

And me?

I was still in high school, still playing ball, still capable of walking either direction.

But the gap between those directions was shrinking.

I had already been in fights. Already felt adrenaline. Already touched the lifestyle. Already seen what came with it. The street life wasn't foreign to me—it was familiar. Comfortable, even.

Sports still gave me peace. But peace doesn't always compete well with excitement. Discipline doesn't always compete well with quick money.

And watching my brothers thrive in their own ways made the streets look less like danger and more like destiny.

"The hardest decisions aren't between right and wrong. They're between what feels good and what lasts."

We had crossed the river once.

Now we were crossing neighborhoods.

But the real movement was happening inside me.

I was no longer just reacting to life.

I was choosing how to live it.

And I could feel that whatever choice I made next wouldn't just shape me.

It would shape the next chapter of our bloodline.

Chapter 8 — High School and The Wight of a Decision

The decision didn't come with fireworks or dramatic music playing in the background. It came quietly, sitting in my chest at seventeen years old, staring at a reality I could not ignore. A pregnant girlfriend. A baby on the way. A responsibility that felt heavier than anything I had ever carried before.

Up until that moment, I had been balancing two identities. I was still in school. I was still playing sports. I was still telling myself I had options. I had watched my brothers move deeper into the streets, and I had been standing on the edge, close enough to see how it worked but not fully committed. I was one chess move away from stepping all the way in. Finding out I was going to be a father made that final move feel inevitable.

Sports suddenly felt uncertain. Practice didn't feel urgent anymore. Games didn't feel like a plan. I wasn't just a kid chasing highlights or hoping for a scholarship. I was about to be responsible for another life. In my seventeen-year-old mind, responsibility translated directly into money. Not long-term planning. Not patience. Not slow growth. Immediate money.

So I quit sports. I told myself it was temporary, that I would come back once things stabilized. But deep down, I knew I had shifted directions.

"Pressure doesn't ask if you're ready. It forces you to respond."

French Quarter Chronicles

I got a job working in the French Quarter. The Quarter exposed me to a different rhythm of life. Tourists walked around carefree, spending money like it would refill itself. Music poured out of bars. Cash flowed from hand to hand without hesitation. I worked my shifts, collected my checks, and tried to convince myself that this would be enough.

But when you're staring at hospital bills, diapers, clothes, and the unknown cost of raising a child, "enough" feels like a moving target.

I started small. I would take a little weed from my brother's stash, nothing major at first, just enough to flip quietly. I justified it by telling myself I was only borrowing opportunity. I wasn't trying to be a kingpin. I wasn't trying to dominate the neighborhood. I was just trying to get by. If someone wanted to buy, I would sell. If the money came, I wasn't going to turn it down.

The first sale I ever made on my own felt bigger than it probably was. It wasn't a huge amount. It wasn't a dramatic handoff. It was simple. A quiet exchange. But I remember the feeling in my chest when I counted the money afterward. It wasn't just about the cash. It was about proving to myself that I could generate income outside of a paycheck. That I could handle responsibility my own way.

I went straight to the store after that first real flip. I didn't buy anything flashy. I bought pampers. I stood in the aisle staring at different sizes, realizing I didn't even know which ones I would need yet. I didn't know if I was having a girl or a boy. That uncertainty made everything feel real. Every time I had a few extra dollars, I would grab something small. A onesie. A tiny pair of socks. A neutral-colored outfit because I didn't know the gender yet. I would look at baby clothes and imagine a future I was trying to build, even if the foundation wasn't solid.

"I was hustling for diapers before I even knew if I was having a son or a daughter."

I wasn't fully submerged in the drug game. Not yet. I didn't wake up thinking about territory or expansion. I still clocked in at work. I still tried to keep my life structured. The hustling was supplemental. It was survival money. But survival money has a way of becoming lifestyle money if you're not careful.

Working in the Quarter helped me move differently. I learned how to blend in. I learned how to talk to people without exposing too much. I understood that discretion was an advantage. If you weren't buying from me, you probably wouldn't know I had anything. I didn't flash money like Lonk. I didn't move aggressively like Baybay. My demeanor stayed calm. Low profile. That was natural for me.

The more I saved, the more confident I became. Eventually, I bought my own pound. Holding it felt like stepping into ownership. This wasn't borrowed product anymore. This was my investment. My risk. My responsibility. I broke it down carefully, measured everything out, planned how it would move. I told myself I would keep it controlled, keep it small, keep it temporary.

But money coming in consistently changes your thinking. Every successful sale reinforced the idea that I was making the right decision. Every time I bought baby clothes or stacked diapers in the corner of the room, I felt justified.

I told myself I wasn't "in the streets." I was just navigating them.

There's a difference in mindset between chasing power and chasing provision. At least that's what I believed. I wasn't trying to build a reputation. I wasn't trying to dominate a block. I just wanted to be prepared when my child arrived. I wanted to look at that baby and know I had done something.

"What felt like responsibility was slowly becoming identity."

As long as the money kept coming, I didn't question it too hard. I wasn't reckless. I wasn't loud. I didn't brag. But the reality was that I had stepped into something that rarely stays small. The neighborhood eventually notices movement. Word travels. And once your name starts circulating—even quietly—it changes how people see you.

At seventeen, I convinced myself I had no choice. I saw the baby as a deadline, a reason to accelerate. But looking back, I realize I still had options. They were just slower. Harder. Less glamorous.

I chose speed.

I chose immediacy.

And even though I told myself it was temporary, every move I made was digging the foundation deeper.

The diapers stacked higher. The clothes piled up in neutral colors. The money flowed just enough to keep me satisfied. I was preparing to be a father, but I was also preparing to be something else entirely.

I thought I was just getting by.

I didn't realize I was building momentum.

And momentum, once it builds, doesn't stop just because your intentions were good.

Counting Down to Fatherhood

As the due date got closer, the pressure stopped feeling abstract and started feeling real. Doctor appointments weren't just check-ins anymore — they were countdown markers. Every visit reminded me that time was moving whether I was ready or not. I would sit in those waiting rooms watching other fathers, wondering if they felt as unprepared as I did. I kept a calm face, but inside I was calculating numbers nonstop. Rent. Pampers. Wipes. Formula. Hospital bills. Unexpected costs I hadn't even considered yet.

I started measuring life differently. Every wasted hour felt expensive. Every missed opportunity to earn felt irresponsible. I wasn't thinking about the long-term consequences of hustling — I was thinking about short-term survival. In my head, this wasn't greed. It was provision.

"When you're about to become a father, fear disguises itself as urgency."

I would leave appointments and go straight to work or straight to make a move. There was no more idle time in my mind. I felt like I was racing against something invisible.

The Diaper Aisle Reality

There's something humbling about standing in the baby aisle at seventeen years old.

I would stare at pampers, trying to figure out sizes, not even knowing what I would need yet. I didn't know if I was having a girl or a boy, so I bought neutral colors. Yellow. Green. White. Every time I had a few extra dollars, I grabbed something small. A onesie. Tiny socks. A little blanket. I would hold the clothes in my hands and imagine a baby small enough to fit inside them.

That's when it would hit me.

This wasn't theoretical anymore.

I was about to be somebody's father.

"I was hustling for diapers before I even knew if I was having a son or a daughter."

Stacking those baby items in my room gave me motivation. It made me feel responsible. It made the money feel justified. I wasn't buying chains. I wasn't buying designer clothes. I was buying survival for someone who hadn't even taken their first breath yet.

That's how I rationalized it.

The Illusion of Control

I convinced myself I wasn't fully in the streets.

I still worked my job in the French Quarter. I still clocked in. I still wore a uniform. I still smiled at customers. I told myself the hustling was temporary — just something to fill the gap.

But every time I made a sale, it became easier.

The first sale felt nervous. My hands were slightly sweaty. My heart beat faster than usual. I kept looking around to make sure nobody was watching. But when the exchange was done and the money was in my hand, the nervousness turned into confidence.

Confidence is dangerous when it grows too quickly.

By the time I bought my first full pound with my own saved money, I felt like I had figured something out. I wasn't loud. I wasn't flashy. If you weren't buying from me, you wouldn't know. I moved calm. I kept my demeanor the same.

But the streets have a way of detecting movement.

"You can move quiet, but your name still travels."

I wasn't trying to build a reputation. I was trying to stay under the radar. But anytime money flows consistently, attention follows eventually.

Provider or Prisoner?

There were nights I would sit alone and stare at the baby clothes stacked in the corner of my room. I would imagine holding my child for the first time and promising them a better life than I had. I meant that promise. I felt it deeply.

What I didn't fully grasp was the contradiction.

I wanted to be present.

But I was stepping into a lifestyle that removes fathers.

"I told myself I was providing. I didn't realize I was gambling with presence."

At seventeen, it felt like I had no choice. It felt like pressure had backed me into a corner. But the truth is, I made a decision. I chose speed over patience. I chose fast money over slow growth. I chose what felt immediate over what might have lasted.

The diapers stacked higher.

The money came quicker.

My confidence grew.

And without realizing it, I was no longer just surviving.

I was building momentum.

And momentum, once it builds in the streets, rarely stops where you planned it to.

Chapter 9 — Guess Who's Home

The Return Before the Ruin

Al had just come home.

Thirteen years gone, and now he was sitting in the living room like he had never left. It felt surreal. He had missed so much — Anthony's death aftermath, our moves, our fights, our growth, our mistakes. Prison had frozen his world while ours kept spinning. Now he was back, trying to find footing in a family that had evolved without him.

There was joy in it, but also adjustment. Freedom is loud when you've been locked away. He walked outside and stood there sometimes, just breathing. Looking at the sky like it was new. Watching cars pass like he was studying how life moved now.

When Al walked back into our lives, it didn't feel like a simple homecoming. It felt like someone stepping out of a time capsule. Thirteen years is a long time to be gone. Long enough for kids to become adults. Long enough for neighborhoods to change names. Long enough for grief to settle into the walls of a house.

He came home leaner. Harder in the eyes. Slower in the way he moved, like he was measuring everything before reacting. Prison changes posture. It changes how you sit. How you look at people. How you listen.

The first few nights, we stayed up late just talking. Or at least listening.

Al had stories.

Not the kind you read in books. The kind that come with pauses in the middle because certain memories don't flow smoothly.

He told us about the fights.

About how in prison, respect isn't optional—it's oxygen. He explained how arguments over small things could escalate instantly. A stare held too long. A misunderstanding in line. A bump in the yard. In there, you don't get the luxury of walking away too many times without it costing you something later.

He described one fight where a guy tried to test him during chow. Said something under his breath. Al let it slide once. The second time, it turned physical. He talked about how fast it happened, how you have to react before you even finish thinking. He wasn't bragging. He was explaining survival.

"In prison, hesitation looks like weakness."

He showed us scars on his knuckles. A small mark near his eyebrow. Evidence of thirteen years of constant alertness.

We didn't get much time to process his return.

Because something bigger was forming in the Gulf.

"Hurricane Katrina"

The Warning We Didn't Respect

The news kept repeating the name: Hurricane Katrina.

Category 5.

The words sounded serious, but hurricanes were part of New Orleans culture. We had seen evacuations before. We had seen storms shift directions before. The city had a rhythm to weather threats, and most of the time, it survived.

We underestimated this one.

My pregnant girlfriend and her family didn't.

They packed early. Loaded up vehicles. Headed to Tennessee without hesitation. I remember standing there watching her leave, knowing she and the baby were safer away from the coast. Part of me wanted to go with them. Another part felt tied to my family. Al had just come home. My mom needed support. It didn't feel right leaving.

So I stayed.

"Sometimes loyalty keeps you in places wisdom would leave."

Landfall

When the storm hit, it didn't arrive politely.

The wind started first — loud, aggressive, relentless. Windows shook. Doors rattled. The sky turned into a gray blur. Rain didn't fall gently; it attacked sideways, slamming into everything in its path. Trees bent in unnatural ways. Debris flew through the air like it had no weight.

Inside the house, we tried to stay calm. We gathered in one room. The power flickered, then went out completely. The silence that followed was heavy. No television. No lights. Just wind screaming outside.

I remember thinking about my unborn child again.

Thinking about whether this was the kind of world I was bringing them into.

"The storm outside matched the uncertainty inside me."

Hours passed, but time didn't feel normal. Every loud bang made us tense. Every gust sounded like it might rip the roof away. Then next thing you know, our roof was gone with the wind. We had survived violence. We had survived poverty. But this felt different. You can't negotiate with wind. You can't reason with water.

We had to kick in the door of the apartment downstairs just for shelter because the rain and wind to much to bare.

When the Water Came

The next day was worse.

It wasn't just the storm — it was the aftermath. The levees failed. News traveled in pieces, in rumors first, then in confirmation. Water was rising. Entire neighborhoods were flooding. The city wasn't just damaged — it was drowning.

Even parts of the Westbank felt the effects. Streets flooded. Access points closed. The air changed. There was a smell — wet, heavy, metallic. Sirens were constant. Helicopters circled overhead. People walked around stunned, trying to process what they were seeing.

New Orleans wasn't functioning anymore.

It was surviving.

"I had seen men destroy parts of my city. I had never seen the city collapse itself."

We had to make decisions quickly. Staying didn't feel safe anymore. Supplies were limited. Gas was scarce. Communication was unreliable. Phones barely worked. You couldn't call people to check on them. You just hoped.

We swam thru water just to go out and loot some supplies that was help get us through the days until the water started to go down. I still couldn't help but to thank about my daughter while I was looting so I picked up a few more boxes of pampers because the ones I had stacked up was soaked in water.

The Superdome Reality

For some of our extended family and friends, the only option was the Caesars Superdome, known then simply as the Superdome. It was supposed to be a refuge of last resort. Instead, it became a symbol of desperation.

We heard stories about it in real time — overcrowded conditions, heat with no proper ventilation, limited food, limited water. Families sleeping on concrete. Babies crying in humid air. Tension building inside the walls of what was once a sports arena.

The Superdome wasn't built for that.

It was built for games.

Now it held fear.

And as I listened to updates and pieced together information, I couldn't stop thinking about how quickly structure disappears when systems fail.

The streets had prepared me for chaos.

But this was systemic collapse.

Displacement

Eventually, we had to leave too.

The roads were a mess. Traffic crawled. People packed whatever they could fit in their vehicles — clothes, documents, children, hope. Some left with nothing but what they could carry.

Driving away from the city felt like betrayal and survival at the same time. I looked back at the skyline, unsure of what would be left when we returned. We had a scare that was worst than the storm. While we was driving one of our tires came off while we driving over 70 mile per hour which caused the car to lean on 2 wheels with sports flying under us as we prayed for our safety again! Not to mention this was a tire we stole off a car at the deanship right down the street from the apartment we was living in, because when our roof came off a lot of nails fell in the area of our vehicle.

Displacement hits different when you've already moved so many times in your life. We had moved from the projects. Moved within Harvey. Now we were being pushed out by nature itself.

"Every time we tried to settle, something uprooted us."

We stayed with relatives temporarily. Crowded houses again. Mattresses on floors again. Shared bathrooms again. It felt familiar, but heavier this time.

Because this wasn't just our struggle.

It was the entire city's.

Separation

Being separated from my pregnant girlfriend during all of this added another layer of anxiety. Communication was inconsistent. I didn't know what the next week would look like, let alone the next month. I was trying to check on my family while also worrying about hers.

The baby was coming whether the city recovered or not.

That reality hit me harder than the storm.

The hustle mindset I had been building before Katrina shifted. Money still mattered, but now survival felt bigger than income. Infrastructure had collapsed. Neighborhoods were underwater. Hustling didn't look the same when customers were displaced across states.

The storm paused everything.

But it didn't reset who we were.

Aftermath and Identity

When we eventually saw the full scope of destruction, it felt unreal. Homes gone. Businesses destroyed. Entire communities erased. Places that held childhood memories were now underwater or condemned.

New Orleans would rebuild.

But it would never be the same.

And neither would we.

"Some storms wash things away. Others reveal what was already fragile."

Al had just come home to freedom, and now the city itself felt imprisoned by water and damage. I was about to become a father in a world that felt unstable at every level. The illusion of control I had built through hustling seemed small compared to the power of nature.

But one thing didn't change.

Pressure.

Pressure to provide.
Pressure to protect.
Pressure to rebuild.

Katrina didn't remove that pressure.

It amplified it.

And as the city slowly tried to stand back up, so did we — carrying trauma from the streets, from loss, and now from disaster.

This wasn't just a hurricane.

It was a reset button that forced everyone to choose who they were going to become next.

And I was standing at another crossroads.

Chapter 10 – Everything's Bigger in Texas

Refugees

They say everything's bigger in Texas.

For us, what felt biggest wasn't the skyline or the highways. It was the word they started calling us.

Refugees.

We weren't tourists. We weren't relocating by choice. We were displaced. Hurricane Katrina had pushed thousands of us across state lines, and Texas became one of the main landing spots. We ended up there navigating a life that didn't feel like ours.

Eventually, a family opened their doors to us. It wasn't luxury. It wasn't space. It was survival. We slept wherever we could fit—floors, sofas, corners of living rooms. Blankets became beds. Privacy disappeared again. But gratitude overpowered discomfort. After what we had just lived through, shelter was enough.

"When you lose everything, even a couch feels like a blessing."

FEMA started distributing assistance. Long lines formed at relief centers. People filled out paperwork with tired eyes and uncertain futures. We received some money, but it wasn't much. It helped, but it didn't rebuild. It didn't replace homes or stability. It didn't quiet the anxiety of not knowing when life would feel normal again.

For a while, everyone was just surviving.

Searching for Opportunity

The younger three of us—me, Lonk, and Baybay—weren't built to sit still for long. Displacement didn't quiet our instincts; it sharpened them. While others waited for assistance, we were scanning the environment differently. We were looking for opportunity. Looking for movement. Looking for a way to turn chaos into leverage.

Texas was new territory, but desperation after the storm created gaps in systems. People were scattered. Supply chains were unstable. Law enforcement was stretched thin. We weren't the only ones thinking about money. Everyone needed it.

My nephew Bill, who earned the name Wild Bill for living recklessly like Baybay, moved with an unpredictable energy. He wasn't cautious. He didn't overthink. If something looked profitable, he stepped toward it fast. That energy connected him with people quickly. And connections were currency.

Bill introduced us to a Spanish-speaking guy who said he had access to kilos of cocaine. At first, it sounded exaggerated. In our world, everybody claims to know somebody with weight. But this was different. The access felt real. The supply felt steady.

When we first heard the word kilos attached to us, it shifted the scale in our minds.

This wasn't flipping ounces.

This was stepping into a different level.

"Small hustles pay bills. Big moves change trajectories."

The Beginning of "Money Money"

The first time we saw that much product in one place, it felt surreal. White bricks stacked neatly. Clean. Organized. Professional. It wasn't street-corner chaos—it was business-level volume. That's when the tone changed between us. The conversations got quieter. The calculations got sharper.

We started smaller than the supply offered. A half kilo at first. It felt safer that way. Easier to manage. Easier to transport. Easier to explain to ourselves.

The money moved faster than anything we had seen before.

Texas was open terrain. New customers. New networks. People displaced from Louisiana still needed what they were used to. And we were positioned between supply and demand.

Soon half a kilo turned into five.

Five turned into ten.

The scale kept expanding because the demand kept answering.

"When opportunity meets hunger, growth comes fast."

The Return Routes

Eventually, the pull of New Orleans became strong again. The city was damaged, but it wasn't dead. People were slowly returning. Reconstruction created movement. With movement comes money.

My mom stayed in Texas for stability, but we started traveling back to New Orleans regularly. At least once a week, we would make the drive. Sundays became our preferred return days because traffic was lighter and there were fewer police on the highways. We studied patterns. We watched rest stops. We paid attention to which routes felt safer.

At first, we transported a half kilo at a time.

Then five.

Then ten.

Every trip carried risk. Every mile felt longer than it was. But the calculations kept making sense financially. The margins were bigger. The turnover faster. The returns heavier.

Everyone needed money after the storm. Insurance claims were slow. Jobs were limited. Reconstruction took time. But ironically, right after Katrina, it was hard to sell anything initially. People were focused on food, shelter, and rebuilding. Luxury spending disappeared. Survival spending dominated.

That forced us to adapt again.

We had to identify who still had access to cash. Contractors. Workers coming into the city. People receiving insurance payouts. Certain neighborhoods rebounded faster than others. The hustle wasn't just about selling—it was about studying economic shifts.

"Disaster destroys structures, but it also rearranges markets."

Dual Lives

We were moving between Texas and Louisiana like we belonged to both and neither. One week displaced sons sleeping on floors. The next week calculated transporters carrying weight across state lines.

I would visit my mom in Texas and see the exhaustion in her eyes. She was grateful we were moving forward, but she didn't fully know how. We didn't talk about details. Some things stayed unspoken.

Then Sunday would come, and we'd be back on the highway headed toward New Orleans. The city still scarred. Buildings boarded up. Neighborhoods half-empty. But opportunity hiding in reconstruction.

The storm had erased so much—but it had also removed certain barriers. Law enforcement was stretched thin. Systems were rebuilding. For people willing to move strategically, gaps existed.

And we filled them.

"We were rebuilding our pockets while the city rebuilt its walls."

Momentum After Disaster

The scale we were operating on now was different from anything I had imagined at seventeen hustling for diaper money. This wasn't survival flipping anymore. This was organized movement. Coordinated transport. Calculated distribution.

And with bigger scale came bigger exposure.

The money stacked higher.

The risks multiplied quietly.

But when you come from nothing and suddenly see large sums consistently, it rewires your perception of normal. What once felt impossible now felt expected.

The storm had displaced us physically.

But financially, it had repositioned us.

And in that repositioning, something changed again inside me.

This wasn't just about providing anymore.

This was about expansion.

"We left as refugees. We returned as operators."

The Drive That Felt Different

The first close call didn't come with gunfire or betrayal.

It came with red and blue lights in the rearview mirror.

By this point, we had already made a few smooth runs between Texas and Louisiana. We had our routine. Sundays were the preferred days—lighter traffic, fewer patrol cars, long stretches of highway that felt predictable. We studied patterns. We convinced ourselves we understood the system.

That confidence is dangerous.

That Sunday felt normal at first. The weight was in the car—more than we had ever transported before. Not a half kilo. Not something small enough to downplay in our minds. This was real volume. Real time. Real consequences if anything went wrong.

We weren't loud. No music blasting. No erratic driving. Seatbelts on. Speeds controlled. We had learned that attention is the enemy.

Somewhere along the highway, I glanced in the side mirror and saw it.

A patrol car.

At first, it was just another vehicle behind us. But it stayed behind us longer than usual. Matched our speed. Changed lanes when we changed lanes. That's when the air inside the car shifted.

Nobody spoke at first.

We all felt it.

"You can't hide fear in a moving car. It fills the silence."

The Lights

Then it happened.

The red and blue lights flashed.

Not subtle.

Not distant.

Directly behind us.

My stomach dropped instantly. Time slowed down in a way that only real fear can cause. Every possible outcome rushed through my head at once. Prison. Charges. Headlines. My daughter growing up without me.

I pulled over carefully, like we had practiced in theory but never actually rehearsed for real. Hands visible. Windows down. Engine off. Breathing controlled.

The weight was in the vehicle.

There was no explaining that away.

"Confidence disappears fast when consequences get real."

The officer approached slowly. Flashlight in hand. Calm voice. He asked for license and registration. I handed them over without shaking, at least not visibly. Inside, my heart was pounding so hard I could feel it in my throat.

He asked where we were coming from.

Texas.

Where were we headed?

New Orleans.

Purpose of travel?

Visiting family.

The answers felt rehearsed even though we had never practiced them out loud.

The Longest Five Minutes

He walked back to his patrol car.

Those five minutes felt like five hours.

Nobody moved. Nobody whispered. You could hear breathing. You could hear the hum of the engine cooling down. You could hear your own thoughts screaming.

Every second stretched. Was he running the plates? Did he smell anything? Did he notice something in our behavior? Had we made a mistake without realizing it?

In those five minutes, I understood something deeply. This wasn't a game anymore. This wasn't hustle for diapers. This was federal time if it went wrong.

"The streets teach you how to move. The highway tests if you've learned."

The Question

The officer returned.

He leaned slightly toward the window and asked if there was anything illegal in the vehicle.

That question hit harder than the lights.

There's a split second in moments like that where your brain tries to evaluate everything—tone, posture, suspicion level. His voice wasn't aggressive. It wasn't accusatory. It was neutral.

I answered calmly.

No, sir.

He stared for a moment longer than comfortable. Then he handed back the paperwork.

Said I had been drifting slightly over the line and to be more careful.

And that was it.

No search. No K-9. No further questions. Just a warning.

After He Drove Off

When he pulled away, none of us celebrated.

Nobody laughed. Nobody bragged.

The silence stayed heavy for miles.

We had just stared at the possibility of everything ending.

And somehow, it didn't.

My hands didn't shake until about ten minutes later. That delayed reaction is real. The body holds tension until it feels safe enough to release it.

I realized something in that moment. We weren't untouchable. We weren't invisible. We were lucky.

And luck runs out.

"Surviving a close call doesn't mean you're safe. It means you were spared."

The Shift

That stop changed me.

Not enough to quit.

But enough to respect the weight of what we were doing.

I drove differently after that. Thought differently. Calculated differently. I understood that one small mistake—one drift across a line, one nervous glance, one inconsistency—could erase everything.

And yet, we kept moving. Because the money was bigger. Because the demand was steady. Because momentum is hard to stop once it builds.

The storm had displaced us.

The hustle had elevated us.

And now, the law had reminded us of the thin line between freedom and a cell.

Al had told stories about prison like it was survivable.

That traffic stop made it feel real.

And for the first time, I truly understood how close I was to repeating his chapter instead of writing my own.

Chapter 11 — When the Money Was Jumping

The City Was Hungry

Right after the storm we picked up where we left off.

When we got back to the city for good, the sales started jumping immediately. It felt like as soon as we touched down with product, it was already spoken for. Reconstruction money was flowing, contractors were everywhere, insurance payouts were finally landing, and people who had been displaced were coming back with cash in their pockets and stress in their systems. Stress creates demand.

Our names started ringing.

We weren't just hustling anymore — we were known as the ones who had the work. Not sometimes. Not occasionally. We had it consistently. That consistency separated us from everybody else trying to move around in the post-storm chaos.

"In a rebuilding city, supply becomes power."

Me and Lonk developed a rhythm. At the end of every week, we would sit down and compare numbers. It wasn't about ego — at least that's what we told ourselves — it was about accountability. Who moved more? Who had stronger clientele? Who needed to tighten up?

Some weeks he would come heavy. Stacks on stacks. Money spread across the table like proof of dominance. Other weeks, I would outpace him quietly, my flow steady and consistent. My customers were loyal.

They appreciated how I handled business. I wasn't loud. I didn't keep them waiting. I didn't create scenes. Discretion was my brand.

Meanwhile, people started whispering that Lonk was drawing too much attention. Flashy money. Obvious movements. Customers feeling uneasy. When you move loud, your clients feel loud too. And in our world, comfort equals retention.

"You don't build a business on noise. You build it on trust."

The Cost at Home

While all this money was being made, something else was deteriorating quietly.

My home life.

My newborn daughter was growing, changing, learning to recognize faces. And I wasn't there enough to see it. I told myself I was doing this for her. Every stack of money I counted, I justified with her name attached to it.

But money doesn't rock babies to sleep.

Money doesn't give mothers rest.

Arguments started small. Little comments at first.

"Why you never home?"

"You said you'd be back earlier."

"I need help."

At first, I brushed it off. Told her she didn't understand the pressure I was under. Told her I was doing this for us. Told her the sacrifice would pay off.

But those little arguments grew teeth.

She would be exhausted, holding the baby all day, needing just a moment to breathe. I would come home late, distracted, sometimes counting money in my head instead of listening. She didn't care about margins. She cared about partnership.

"You always running the streets."

"You need to be here."

"I can't do this by myself."

Her words weren't dramatic. They were tired.

And tired turns into resentment fast.

"I was providing financially but absent emotionally."

We started fighting about everything. Dishes. Phone calls. Time. Tone. The little things became symbols of bigger problems. She wasn't arguing about laundry. She was arguing about presence.

And deep down, I knew she was right.

But I wasn't ready to step back.

The Table Turned

Back to the money.

The weekly sit-downs with Lonk started shifting. The first time he came to the table light, I didn't think much of it. Everybody has slow weeks. The second time, it caught my attention. The third time, it was clear something was wrong.

He started coming with less and less re-up money.

I was still moving steady. My flow hadn't slowed. My clientele stayed loyal. But he was struggling to keep up. Whether it was attention, distractions, or internal issues, his consistency faded.

Two weeks in a row, he came to the table with nothing.

Nothing.

That silence at the table hit harder than any argument we'd ever had. I wasn't angry at first — I was calculating. If he couldn't contribute, the scale of the operation shifted entirely onto me.

That's when I told him something that changed our dynamic.

I told him I would keep his name alive, but I had to handle it on my own.

"Sometimes loyalty means carrying someone. Sometimes it means separating."

He went broke.

Flat broke.

While I kept hustling.

Alone in the Field

For months, I was out there by myself.

No shared splits. No joint calculations. Just me moving weight and keeping the operation afloat. The pressure increased, but so did the control. I no longer had to adjust to someone else's mistakes. Every move was mine. Every decision was mine.

And because of that, I built my own crew.

It wasn't random.

It was strategic.

A few of my potnas from the Westbank — guys who understood discipline. Some from Uptown — who knew movement and territory. A few from Downtown — who brought connections and reach.

I didn't recruit based on hype. I recruited based on reliability.

"You don't build a crew on friendship. You build it on performance."

The operation expanded. My name stopped being attached to "us" and started being attached to "me." That came with pride. It also came with exposure.

At the same time, my daughter was growing.

Her mother was growing more distant.

And I was growing deeper into something that was no longer just temporary hustle.

The Trade-Off

There's a dangerous feeling that comes with carrying everything successfully. It makes you believe you were meant for it. That you're built different. That you can handle scale alone.

The money stacked higher than it ever had.

But the arguments at home stacked higher too.

I was building an empire in the streets while my foundation at home cracked slowly.

"Success in one area doesn't cancel failure in another."

And even though I told myself this was all for my family, I was slowly becoming a stranger inside my own house.

The city knew my name.

But my daughter barely knew my presence.

And I was too focused on winning the week to realize what I was losing long-term.

As months passed and Lonk faded out of the day-to-day movement, someone else naturally stepped into position.

One of my closest friends — my right-hand man — started riding with me more often. At first, it was just company on the road. Long highway drives are different when you're carrying weight. Silence gets louder. Thoughts get heavier. Having someone you trust in the passenger seat changes the energy.

Before long, he wasn't just riding.

He was participating.

We started moving like Lonk and I used to move — coordinated, synced, aware of each other's strengths. He understood discretion. He didn't talk too much. He didn't brag. He moved with purpose. That mattered to me.

"Trust is the real currency when you're carrying risk."

The first few runs together felt like tests. Not of the route — of the bond. Could he handle pressure? Would he stay calm if something unexpected happened? Would he fold under stress?

He didn't.

On the highway, we developed our own rhythm. Windows slightly cracked. Music low. Conversations controlled. We talked about business, about scaling smarter, about avoiding the mistakes we had seen others make. There was ambition in those drives. Not reckless ambition — strategic ambition.

He became my sounding board.

My second set of eyes.

My confirmation when something felt off.

Becoming "Us"

Over time, me and him became what me and Lonk once were.

Two operators moving in sync.

We would split responsibilities naturally. He handled certain connections. I handled others. He managed certain logistics. I oversaw bigger decisions. There was no loud declaration about partnership — it just evolved.

Money started flowing through both of us consistently. When you build something with someone from the ground up, there's a different level of loyalty that forms. It's not just about profit. It's about shared risk.

"Partnership in the streets isn't about friendship. It's about shared silence."

We didn't need to say everything out loud. A look was enough. A nod was enough. That kind of chemistry is rare.

And it was dangerous.

Because once you find someone who matches your pace and your thinking, scaling becomes easier.

The Highway Brotherhood

The drives became longer.

The loads became heavier.

The confidence grew.

Sometimes we would sit in the car before pulling off, just looking straight ahead, both knowing what was sitting in the trunk or hidden in the panels. There's a moment before every risky move where time pauses slightly. That pause bonds people.

On the road, we talked about expansion. About moving smarter. About not repeating patterns we had seen destroy others. We critiqued other crews. We analyzed mistakes. We believed we were operating differently.

Calculated.

Disciplined.

Low profile.

"Every crew thinks they're the exception until reality reminds them."

We built trust not just through money, but through consistency. He showed up when he said he would. He handled situations calmly. He didn't chase spotlight.

That made me comfortable.

Too comfortable.

The Growth

With him beside me, the operation grew stronger. The crew tightened. Distribution got smoother. My name was ringing, but his started echoing alongside mine.

It felt like a new chapter.

No longer tied to my brothers' shadow.

No longer dependent on anyone unreliable.

Just two men moving strategically in a city rebuilding itself.

But there's something about success that makes you forget the fragility of it.

Money was flowing.

Respect was building.

Power was expanding.

And in the middle of all of it, I was still fighting at home. Still arguing about time. Still missing milestones. Still convincing myself that once I hit a certain number, I would slow down.

"We kept telling ourselves one more run. One more week. One more stack."

But the street never accepts "just one more."

And the deeper we moved together, the more inevitable something felt.

Because history had already shown me something.

Every time I thought I had control… Life shifted!

Chapter 12 — Revolving Door

The First Arrest

Baybay's first serious arrest didn't come with drama or a high-speed chase. It came during a routine traffic stop, the kind that most people barely think about. But in our world, traffic stops were never minor inconveniences — they were moments where everything could unravel in seconds. He was pulled over, and drugs were found in the car. Once that happened, there was no negotiating, no smooth talking, no escaping the reality of what came next. Handcuffs closed around his wrists, and just like that, he was gone.

When we got the news, it didn't feel shocking. It felt inevitable. Baybay had been moving aggressively for a while. His energy had shifted from reckless to confrontational, and that kind of presence eventually draws attention whether you intend it to or not. My mom reacted the way she always did — quietly. She didn't scream. She didn't break down publicly. She absorbed it. I could see the disappointment in her eyes, but even more than that, I could see exhaustion.

"When jail becomes familiar, disappointment turns into fatigue."

He did his time and eventually came home. For a brief period, there was hope that the experience might have slowed him down. At first, he moved cautiously. He stayed close to the house. He tried to adjust. But prison hadn't scared him — it had hardened him. It sharpened the edge that was already there. He came back more intense, more impatient, less willing to tolerate disrespect.

And then it happened again.

He would come home for a year or two, try to regain his footing, and then slowly drift back into the same patterns. The same fast money. The same risky decisions. The same aggressive responses. Each time he went back in, the emotional reaction in our house became more muted on the surface but heavier underneath. It felt like watching someone step into a revolving door that wouldn't stop spinning.

"Some people survive jail. Others adapt to it."

Over time, incarceration stopped feeling like an interruption and started feeling like part of the lifestyle. That realization scared me more than the arrests themselves. When prison becomes expected, something in the environment is broken at a deeper level. And even though I was still free, I couldn't ignore that the pattern was tightening around our family.

Pressure and Pride

While Baybay was cycling in and out of jail, Lonk was dealing with a different kind of pressure. His identity had been built on reputation, consistency, and dominance. When his money had slowed down before, it bruised more than his pockets — it bruised his pride. He had an image to uphold, and that image required visible strength. Over time, the stress of rebuilding that reputation began to show. His patience shortened. His tolerance for perceived disrespect disappeared.

Anyone who owed him money felt the pressure immediately. What might have once been handled with conversation now carried tension. Even something as small as a look that felt wrong could escalate faster than it should have. In environments like ours, pride can distort perception, and once perception shifts, reaction follows.

"When your name becomes your identity, every interaction feels like a challenge."

The Argument Downtown

The incident outside Harrah's New Orleans unfolded on a night that should have been ordinary. The casino lights were bright, people were moving in and out dressed for entertainment, and downtown carried its usual buzz. I was inside and Lonk stopped at the house and asked was I coming outside to the club with him. Something told me not to, and that something was right.

An argument started — something about money, something about pride. It could have ended with words. It didn't.

The exchange escalated. Voices grew louder. Tension tightened. And then shots rang out. The sound cut through the night, sharp and final. People screamed. Tires screeched against pavement. In seconds, what had been an argument turned into chaos. One man went down. A truck pulled away fast, disappearing into traffic.

Witnesses called police immediately. Descriptions went out quickly over scanners — two Black males fleeing the scene in a large truck. And that truck happened to belong to Lonk and one of our potnas.

At first, it seemed like they had gotten away. Downtown at night is chaotic enough to create momentary cover. But cameras don't panic. Witnesses don't forget. And police pressure intensifies fast when violence happens in visible public spaces. It wasn't long before officers located the vehicle and cornered them. There was no dramatic final escape. Just flashing lights from multiple directions and nowhere left to go.

The Weight of the Pattern

When I got the call, the weight of it hit differently than Baybay's arrest. This wasn't just possession. This wasn't a cycle of short stays. This was serious. This was violence with consequences that could stretch years.

"One emotional decision can erase years of calculated movement."

As I sat alone processing everything, I couldn't ignore the pattern forming around me. Anthony had been lost to the streets. Al had lost thirteen years. Baybay was trapped in a revolving door. Now Lonk was facing time that could reshape his future entirely. And I was still out there, still moving, still convincing myself that I was different because I was more calculated.

But calculation doesn't make you immune.

It just delays the lesson.

"You can think you're smarter than the cycle. Until the cycle reaches for you."

For the first time, I wasn't just afraid of getting caught. I was afraid of becoming predictable — another branch of the same story repeating itself. And that realization sat heavier than any stack of money ever had.

Chapter 13 — The Moment I Couldn't Ignore

All My Brothers Gone

There came a moment when the noise around me quieted just enough for the truth to get loud. Lonk was gone. Baybay was gone. Al was gone. Every one of my brothers was back in jail at the same time. I remember sitting alone with that realization and feeling something shift inside of me. Growing up, no matter how chaotic things were, I was never alone in it. There was always one of them around, even if only by phone. Now the silence felt different. It wasn't just physical absence; it was the weight of pattern.

I could only imagine how my mom felt. She had already buried one son. Now the other three more were locked away. I thought about how she carried grief quietly, how she had learned to process heartbreak without showing too much of it. The idea that all her boys were either gone or headed down the same road had to sit heavy on her chest at night. I started seeing her not just as my mother, but as a woman who had endured more loss than most people survive emotionally.

"A mother doesn't just lose sons to prison. She loses pieces of herself."

And I was still out there.

Still moving.

Still free.

Money and the Mirror

The money was coming in heavy during that time. Sales were steady. My name carried weight. There was recognition attached to my presence. Women wanted me or they want the image of me and they wanted what I could do for them. People respected how I moved. From the outside, it looked like success. I had everything the streets promise —cash flow, status, control.

But one night, after counting a stack of money at my table, I found myself staring at it longer than usual. Instead of feeling pride, I felt something else rising in me. A question that I had avoided for years.

Do I really want this life?

It wasn't panic. It wasn't fear in the dramatic sense. It was clarity creeping in slowly. Yes, I was earning. Yes, I had notoriety. Yes, there was attention and validation. But at what cost? I was too smart to ignore the pattern forming around me. Anthony was gone. Al had lost thirteen years. Baybay kept going in and out. Lonk had just been locked up for something serious. The signs weren't subtle anymore.

"When every warning sign points in one direction, pretending not to see it becomes a decision."

I could no longer claim ignorance. I understood cause and effect. I understood momentum. And I understood that I was not immune.

The Pressure at Home

While all this was unfolding, home was unraveling quietly. The mother of my daughter was exhausted, and her exhaustion didn't come with screaming or threats. It came with frustration that built slowly over time. She would tell me I was never home. That she needed help. That our daughter needed more than financial support. I would respond defensively at first, explaining the pressure I was under, reminding her that I was doing this for our child.

But deep down, I knew she wasn't asking for money. She was asking for presence.

Arguments started small and grew bigger. It wasn't about one specific issue. It was about absence. It was about responsibility. It was about partnership. I was providing financially, but I wasn't emotionally available. I would come home distracted, still mentally counting what I made or planning the next move. She was living in real time with a newborn, and I was living in survival mode.

"Money can pay bills, but it can't replace presence."

And every time she cried out of frustration, it chipped away at whatever justification I had built for myself.

The Weight of Paranoia

Sending money to my brothers in jail was the easy part. That was transactional. I could deposit funds into commissary accounts without stepping into danger. It felt like I was doing my duty as a brother. But actually going to visit them felt different. Walking into a jail while actively selling drugs created a level of paranoia that I couldn't shake. Every time I thought about going, my mind ran through scenarios. What if someone was watching me? What if my name had already been flagged? What if I walked in and didn't walk back out?

Every police car on the road felt intentional. Every unfamiliar face felt observant. A knock at the door made my heart race for a split second longer than it should have. I started realizing that paranoia was replacing peace in my life. I was constantly alert, constantly scanning, constantly calculating.

"When paranoia becomes normal, you're already paying a price."

The money still came, but it didn't feel as clean. It didn't feel as empowering. It felt heavy.

The Truth I Couldn't Dodge

One night, I forced myself to look at everything honestly. I had always told myself I was different from my brothers because I was more disciplined, more strategic, more controlled. I wasn't reckless. I didn't let emotion drive my decisions. But intelligence doesn't cancel consequences. Being calculated doesn't make you invincible.

The hardest realization wasn't that I might get caught. It was admitting that I wasn't trapped. I wasn't forced into this life anymore. I was choosing it. I liked the money. I liked the control. I liked the validation. That truth hurt more than any external threat.

"Sometimes the hardest truth is admitting you're not stuck — you're comfortable."

All my brothers were behind bars. My daughter was growing every day. My mom was carrying a grief that didn't get lighter with time. And I was still balancing on the same edge, convincing myself I could outsmart the fall.

Bloodline or Breakline

For the first time, I didn't just fear jail. I feared repetition. I feared becoming another predictable chapter in the same story. I imagined my daughter growing up explaining where her father was. I imagined her normalizing absence the way I had normalized chaos. That thought hit deeper than fear of prison ever could.

The streets had given me money, recognition, and movement. But they had also taken brothers, time, peace, and stability. I started to understand that breaking a cycle requires more than awareness. It requires action. And action often means walking away from something that feels powerful.

"Cycles don't end because you notice them. They end when you step out of them."

That night, I didn't have all the answers. I didn't suddenly transform. But the question had finally taken root in me. And once you truly question a life you've been living, it becomes impossible to move the same way without feeling the weight of that awareness.

This was the moment I could no longer pretend I didn't see it.

The moment where everything — money, reputation, pride — stood on one side.

And legacy stood on the other.

Chapter 14 — The Moment I Couldn't Ignore

The Breaking Point I Didn't Share

Things were becoming overwhelming, but I didn't tell anyone. I've always been a man who speaks sparingly. I don't waste words, and I don't confide easily. When I do speak, it carries weight. People listen because they know I don't talk just to hear myself. But during this time, I kept everything internal. The pressure, the paranoia, the pattern unfolding around me — I carried it alone.

Late one night, after another long day of movement and money, I sat by myself and said something out loud that I hadn't admitted to anyone else. I didn't whisper it in fear. I didn't say it dramatically. I said it calmly, intentionally, like I was signing a contract with my own conscience.

"This is the last run."

Once I move these last bricks, I'm shutting it down.

And I meant it.

I wasn't reacting emotionally. I wasn't scared in the moment. I was aware. All my brothers were back in jail. My mom had already endured more than any mother should. My daughter was growing, and I was watching milestones through exhaustion instead of presence. The paranoia had started creeping into places it never used to reach. I could feel the walls closing in — not physically, but spiritually.

"When clarity arrives, it doesn't yell. It settles quietly in your chest."

I believed I had enough stacked to pivot. Enough to transition. Enough to walk away before the streets decided my fate for me. I convinced myself I was leaving on my own terms.

The Routine That Didn't Raise Alarms

There was a client I had been serving consistently for a while. He wasn't loud, wasn't flashy, and didn't ask unnecessary questions. He moved with calm energy, which made him easy to deal with. Twice a week, he would grab nine ounces of cocaine. That was our pattern. It was steady, predictable, and professional. Nothing about it felt unstable.

When he called and told me to meet him at the spot, it didn't feel unusual. The spot was IHOP parking lot — neutral territory. Public enough to blend in, casual enough not to draw suspicion. We had used similar locations before. There was comfort in familiarity.

I pulled up. He walked over calmly. No tension in his body language. No hesitation in his tone. He grabbed the usual amount and left. I left shortly after. It felt routine, almost mechanical. Just another transaction in a long list of transactions that had gone smoothly.

A few days later, he called again. His voice was steady, but this time he asked for something different. Instead of nine ounces, he wanted a half kilo. That was a jump. Not outrageous, but bigger than his norm. For a brief second, something flickered in my mind — a question about why the sudden increase. But I brushed it off. He had been reliable. He had the money. The business relationship had been consistent.

So I provided it.

He took it and went about his business the same way he always had. Calm. Composed. No unusual signals.

What I didn't know was that nothing about this was routine anymore.

"The most dangerous setups don't feel like traps. They feel like patterns."

The Invisible Investigation

Every time I completed a transaction with him, federal agents were watching.

They weren't obvious. There were no dramatic moments of cars screeching or flashing lights trailing me. They were patient. They were methodical. They were building something slowly while I believed I was moving clean.

After each meet, they tracked my vehicle. They followed my movements. They documented my routes. They paid attention to where I went once the transaction was finished.

And I didn't make it difficult for them.

Because after every sale, I went home.

Not to stash product in some elaborate hiding place. Not to meet more clients immediately. I went home because I was trying to be present in my daughter's life. I would park in the same area. Walk into the same residence. Follow the same routine. What I thought was balance — hustling and then returning to fatherhood — became predictability.

"I thought going home proved I wasn't lost. It made me easy to find."

They studied my comfort. They studied my consistency. They studied my sense of security.

While I was planning my exit, they were constructing their case.

The False Calm

After that half-kilo transaction, I remember feeling a strange sense of relief. The move had gone smoothly. The money was clean. The exchange had felt normal. I told myself again that this was almost over. Just a few more transactions and I would walk away.

I started mentally organizing my next chapter. I imagined reducing exposure. Transitioning into legitimate streams. Being more present at home. Breaking the cycle that had swallowed my brothers one by one. I felt like I was ahead of the inevitable.

But there's something cruel about timing.

You can decide you're done with the streets.

That doesn't mean the streets are done with you.

"Sometimes clarity arrives right before consequence."

I had no idea that every move I made that week was being logged. Every mile tracked. Every meet documented. What felt like control was actually the final stage of a trap closing in slowly.

The Night Before

The night before everything shifted, I held my daughter longer than usual. She didn't know about weight, paranoia, surveillance, or promises made in silence. She just knew her father. I remember looking at her and feeling both pride and guilt at the same time. Pride that I had provided. Guilt that I had risked too much to do it.

In my head, I repeated it again.

This is the last run.

After this, I'm done.

I believed it.

But belief doesn't stop momentum.

And momentum, once it builds in this life, rarely slows down because you've had a moment of reflection.

I didn't get out in time.

And the promise I made to myself would soon collide with reality in a way I couldn't control.

The Morning That Still Haunts Me

I remember that morning as clearly as if it were happening right now. July 23, 2009 is a date that has never faded from my memory. Some days blur over time, but that day never has. It replays in my mind with full detail — the sounds, the light coming through the window, even the feeling in my chest before everything changed.

It was early, around 8:00 in the morning. I was sitting on the sofa watching *SportsCenter*. Sports had never left my system. No matter how far I drifted from the version of myself that once dreamed through athletics, I still found comfort in highlights and analysis. Watching those athletes compete reminded me of discipline, structure, and focus — things I once had and slowly replaced with something else.

The house was calm. It felt like any other ordinary morning.

And then the bang came.

It wasn't a knock. It wasn't someone tapping politely at the door. It was a violent impact that shook the walls and shattered the stillness. Before my mind could fully process the sound, voices followed.

"Open up! Open up! Everybody get on the ground!"

The commands were loud, sharp, and urgent. It all happened so quickly that my body reacted before my thoughts could catch up. I remember trying to stand, but my legs felt heavy, almost numb. It wasn't that I consciously chose not to run. It was like something inside me understood that running wasn't an option.

"When reality finally catches you, your body feels it before your pride accepts it."

The Warrant With My Name On It

They flooded into the house with precision. Tactical gear. Controlled movement. Weapons drawn but steady. This wasn't local officers responding to chaos. This was organized. Planned. Executed with confidence.

One of the agents stepped toward me and announced they had a federal warrant for the house. He spoke calmly, like this was routine. Like this was another item on a list.

Then he said something that hit harder than the door ever could.

They had been investigating.

And they were finally coming to get me.

I remember looking at him and saying, almost instinctively, "Me? You sure?"

It wasn't arrogance. It wasn't denial in the dramatic sense. It was disbelief. In my mind, I had been quiet. I wasn't loud in the streets. I didn't flash money recklessly. I operated with discretion. I convinced myself that calculated movement meant protection.

He looked at me and asked, "You're Brennan Jacques, right?"

There was no room left for confusion.

In that moment, something inside me went still. I leaned back into the sofa and stopped speaking. The illusion of control that I had held onto for so long evaporated instantly.

"The second your name is called in a warrant, the game is over."

The Search

They began tearing through the house with a level of focus that made it clear this wasn't random. Drawers were pulled open. Closets emptied. Cushions flipped. Boxes opened. Every square inch examined. The sounds of objects being moved, tossed aside, and inspected felt louder than the initial entry.

Meanwhile, my phone began ringing repeatedly. Word travels quickly when federal vehicles pull up in a neighborhood. People who saw the activity outside were already calling to see if it was true. Associates. Friends. Curious onlookers.

The agents ignored the first few calls and let the phone ring. Then it rang again. And again.

Finally, one particular number came through, and one of the agents looked at the screen and told me to answer it. At the time, I didn't fully understand why that call mattered. I answered, trying to keep my voice steady. The conversation was brief. Controlled. Nothing dramatic.

Later, when I replayed it in my head, I realized what had likely happened. That caller was the confidential informant. The person who had been working with them. The person who wanted confirmation that they had the right man in custody.

The setup had been in motion long before that morning.

"The trap doesn't start when they knock. It starts when you feel comfortable."

"Bingo"

As they continued searching, their voices began to shift in tone.

"Bingo, I found something over here."

"Bingo, I got some money on this side."

Each discovery was announced like a milestone. I watched as they pulled out evidence and placed it on tables. I watched as they high-fived each other. I watched as they smiled.

To them, it was a successful operation. Months of surveillance validated. Paperwork justified. Hours invested rewarded.

To me, it was my life unraveling in real time.

What they called evidence, I saw as consequences stacking in front of me. Every dollar represented a decision. Every item they recovered symbolized a step deeper into a life I had promised myself I was about to leave.

"What they celebrated as a win, I felt as collapse."

The Numbness

I expected to feel panic. I expected anger. I expected something explosive inside of me.

Instead, I felt numb.

Completely numb.

It was as if my mind shut down emotion to shield me from the weight of the moment. I sat there quietly while strangers dismantled my space and prepared to dismantle my freedom.

My thoughts drifted to my daughter. I thought about her small hands and how I had held her just nights before. I thought about my mother, who had already lost one son to death and three more to incarceration at different times. And then I thought about the promise I had made to myself.

This is the last run.

I had said it out loud. I had meant it. I truly believed I was walking away.

But belief doesn't undo momentum.

"Sometimes clarity comes right before consequence."

The Walk Outside

When they placed the handcuffs around my wrists, the metal felt colder than I expected. Not physically painful, but heavy with meaning. They walked me outside, and I noticed curtains shifting in nearby homes. Neighbors peeking through windows. Silent witnesses to what was happening.

The same reputation that once made me feel powerful now made me feel exposed. The same streets I had navigated confidently now felt like spectators to my downfall.

I kept my head steady. I didn't resist. I didn't speak much. The weight of what was happening had already settled in.

"Reputation feels powerful until it becomes public."

The Ride

Sitting in the back of the vehicle, I watched the city pass by through tinted windows. Streets I had driven countless times looked unfamiliar. Familiar turns felt distant. The illusion that I had mastered my environment dissolved with every mile.

I realized something in that ride.

I wasn't smarter than the cycle.

I wasn't immune to repetition.

I had seen the signs. I had questioned the life. I had even tried to exit. But hesitation cost me.

And July 23, 2009 became the day the illusion officially ended.

Chapter 15 — The Interrogation

The Room Where It Became Real

The interrogation room looked exactly like something you would see in a movie, but there was nothing cinematic about the feeling of sitting inside it. The space was small and intentionally plain, with a metal table bolted to the floor and chairs positioned in a way that made it clear who controlled the room. The fluorescent lights hummed above, creating an almost sterile atmosphere that made everything feel official and irreversible. There were no windows, no distractions, just walls and the quiet understanding that this was where truth and consequence would meet.

I walked in still numb. The shock of the morning hadn't fully settled yet. I couldn't believe that federal agents had been building a case against me. In my mind, I had been careful. I wasn't loud. I didn't broadcast my movement. I kept things discreet. But clearly, my name had been traveling further than I understood. My reputation had reached ears I didn't even know were listening.

"You don't always hear your name ringing the way the world does."

When the agents entered the room, they weren't aggressive or hostile. Their calmness carried more weight than shouting ever could. They spoke in measured tones, explaining that I had options. They talked about cooperation. They framed it strategically, almost like they were offering me an opportunity instead of presenting consequences. They asked whether I wanted to help myself. They suggested that there was no reason to carry ten years when I could possibly reduce it by providing information. They questioned why I would protect people who might not protect me in return. The words weren't loud, but they were deliberate.

I sat there quietly, listening, but still processing the fact that I was even in that position. I wasn't ready to respond because I was still trying to understand how I had gone from believing I was moving carefully to sitting in a federal interrogation room.

The Indictment in Black and White

When they placed the indictment in front of me, everything shifted from abstract to concrete. Seeing my name printed on federal paperwork, accompanied by charges and potential years attached to each count, felt different from any street rumor or speculation. The language was structured and precise. Dates were listed. Locations were documented. Quantities were detailed. It wasn't chaotic or exaggerated; it was organized.

As I read through the pages, I began to piece together the timeline in my own mind. Meeting locations. Transaction amounts. Specific days that I could now recall with uncomfortable clarity. I started to understand how long the investigation had been unfolding without my awareness. This wasn't random enforcement. This was surveillance layered over a few weeks.

"You think you're moving quietly until you see your movements typed out in court language."

My thoughts went immediately back to the morning of the raid, when my phone kept ringing while I was sitting in handcuffs on the floor. At the time, the call that they insisted I answer didn't fully register. In the interrogation room, it did. The pattern in the indictment showed repeated meetings at familiar parking lots, specific times that lined up with one person consistently. There was only one name that matched every detail. The only person who would meet me at IHOP parking lots without hesitation. The only one who had recently increased his orders. The only one who had the access and opportunity.

That was when it became clear. He had been wired. They had audio. They had video surveillance of the last transactions. The meetings that felt routine were documented. The conversations that felt private were recorded.

"The setup wasn't loud. It was recorded patiently."

Federal, Not Parish

Local charges carry one type of weight. Federal charges carry another entirely. Sitting there reading through the indictment, I understood that this wasn't a case built on suspicion. It was constructed with intention. Federal agents do not move forward unless the evidence aligns. They do not raid homes unless the paperwork is tight. They do not present indictments without layers.

This wasn't Orleans Parish. This wasn't something that might dissolve with negotiation or technicality. This was federal prison being discussed in a calm, measured tone across a metal table.

The agents continued circling back to cooperation, framing it as a smart move. They spoke about sentencing guidelines, percentages, and the possibility of reducing time. Their approach wasn't emotional. It was mathematical. It was about numbers, not loyalty. They wanted expansion of their case. They wanted information that extended beyond me.

I sat there quietly, absorbing everything, realizing that the illusion of control I had maintained for years had officially ended. I had thought I was operating strategically. In reality, I had been studied strategically.

"I didn't just get arrested. I was calculated."

The Transfer

It wasn't long before I was moved from Orleans Parish Prison to St. Charles Parish, to a tier specifically designated for federal inmates who were awaiting court proceedings or transport to federal facilities. The shift in environment was immediate. The conversations were different. The atmosphere was heavier. Men on that tier weren't discussing minor charges or short-term stays. They were discussing federal time, plea agreements, sentencing ranges, and release percentages.

Walking onto that tier felt like crossing an invisible line. Parish jail holds you temporarily. The federal system processes you systematically. The men there understood that once you enter the federal system, timelines become structured and predictable. There is less flexibility. Less uncertainty. More calculation.

Sitting there replaying everything in my mind—the IHOP parking lot exchanges, the phone call I answered while in handcuffs—I began to see how the pieces had aligned against me. What I once believed was controlled distribution was actually documented evidence. What I thought was routine business had become a timeline in a federal case.

All my brothers had done time in their own ways. Now I was stepping into mine. Not because I was less intelligent. Not because I was reckless. But because I believed I could exit before consequences arrived.

"I said this would be the last run, and it was—just not on my terms."

Sitting in that cell, waiting for what came next, I finally understood something that had been chasing me for years. The streets don't end when you decide they should. They end when the system decides you've had enough time to move freely.

And by then, it's no longer your decision!

Walking Into Reality

As I stepped onto that federal tier, the first thing that hit me wasn't fear — it was weight. The sound of the metal doors closing behind me echoed in a way that felt permanent. The air inside was different from parish jail. It wasn't chaotic. It wasn't loud in the same way. It was structured. Controlled. Heavy with men who already knew their numbers.

All I could think about was my daughter and my mom.

Everything else — the charges, the paperwork, the agents — faded for a second. What stayed clear in my mind was the image of my little girl and the reality of my mother sitting somewhere trying to process that every one of her sons was locked up at the same time.

Baybay had already been gone for over a year, serving a five-year sentence. Lonk had just gone to trial and been convicted on an attempted murder charge. He was only a few months into a twelve-year sentence. Al had violated his parole and was backing up the remainder of a ten-year probation stretch. And then there was me — the last one — facing ten years federally for possession with intent to distribute crack and cocaine.

All her boys.

Gone.

"A mother can survive poverty. I don't know how she survives watching all her sons disappear behind bars."

The Numbers

On that tier, numbers are currency. Men don't ask, "What happened?" They ask, "How much time you got?" The answer isn't emotional. It's mathematical. 120 months. 180 months. 60 months. You say it like you're announcing a contract.

I sat on that metal bunk thinking about the irony of it all. They had seized my vehicle. They had taken almost $100,000 in cash. They had frozen my bank accounts. Everything material I had built was wiped away in one coordinated move. Cars, money, accounts — gone.

But strangely, I wasn't thinking about the loss of those things.

I wasn't worried about the vehicle.

I wasn't worried about the money.

I wasn't even thinking about the frozen accounts.

I was thinking about how my daughter would understand this one day.

I was thinking about my mom sitting somewhere replaying every moment of raising us, wondering where it all went wrong.

"They took my money in one day. I had been losing my freedom for years."

The Pattern Made Visible

Lying there staring at the ceiling, I couldn't escape the pattern anymore. Anthony gone. Al locked up. Baybay locked up. Lonk locked up. And now me. It wasn't coincidence. It wasn't bad luck. It wasn't random targeting.

It was a cycle. Trauma in the Bloodline

And I had walked into it fully aware of the signs.

I had told myself I was smarter. I had convinced myself I was more calculated. I believed I would exit before consequence arrived. But stepping onto that federal tier erased that illusion. Intelligence without discipline is just delayed destruction.

For the first time, I didn't feel anger at the system. I didn't feel rage at the informant. I didn't even feel bitterness about the seizure of everything I had accumulated.

I felt responsibility.

"At some point, you stop blaming the storm and realize you kept walking into it."

The Hardest Thought

The hardest thought wasn't about prison time. It wasn't about percentages or release dates. It was imagining my daughter growing up with a father behind bars. It was imagining her asking questions about why I wasn't there. It was imagining her visiting rooms, metal detectors, and scheduled phone calls instead of school drop-offs and bedtime stories.

I thought about my mom having to answer questions from people in the neighborhood. I thought about her walking into visitation rooms for the fourth time in her life, sitting across from another son in a uniform.

Material loss didn't hurt.

Legacy did.

"Money can be seized. Time cannot be returned."

The Shift

As the night settled in and the tier quieted down, something shifted inside of me. Not dramatically. Not loudly. But firmly. I realized that for the first time, I wasn't worried about reputation. I wasn't worried about image. I wasn't worried about what people would say.

I was worried about what my family felt.

I was worried about how many more cycles could repeat if I didn't change something at the core.

All my brothers were incarcerated.

And I was the last one who could decide whether this story would continue or finally end with me.

Sitting on that bunk, staring at concrete walls, I understood something I had avoided for years.

This wasn't about money anymore.

This was about bloodline.

And whether I was going to continue it — or break it.

Chapter 16 — Sentencing

87 to 108 Months

When it was time for sentencing, everything felt slower than it actually was. By that point, I had already read my paperwork so many times that the numbers were burned into my mind. My guideline range was between 87 and 108 months. I understood what that meant technically. I had learned the math of the federal system. I knew how guidelines worked. I knew about percentages. I knew about good time credits.

But knowing numbers on paper and hearing them spoken in a courtroom are two completely different experiences.

Standing there in front of the judge, I felt a strange calm. I had already accepted responsibility. There was no point pretending. There was no more denial. I knew what I had done. I knew how I got there.

The judge acknowledged that this was my first federal conviction. He spoke about guidelines, about accountability, about deterrence. Then he announced that he was giving me the bottom of my guideline range.

Eighty-seven months.

I'm good with numbers. Always have been. I can calculate quickly in my head. But in that moment, I couldn't even convert it into years. My brain didn't want to process it. I just heard "months" and felt the weight of time settle on my shoulders.

"When a judge speaks in months, your life translates it into years."

I nodded. I didn't argue. I didn't react outwardly. I had already prepared myself for worse. The bottom of the guideline felt like mercy in a system that rarely gives it.

Shipped Out

Not long after sentencing, I was shipped to Federal Correctional Institution, Beaumont Low in Texas. The ride there felt like a transfer not just of location, but of identity. Parish jail had been temporary. The federal holding facility had been transitional. Beaumont was reality.

Five years of my life would be spent there.

Walking into Beaumont felt intimidating at first. Every prison has its own culture, its own rhythm, its own rules that aren't written anywhere official. As I stepped inside, I scanned the environment instinctively. Faces. Body language. Movement. You learn quickly to read rooms when your safety depends on it.

What surprised me was seeing familiar faces. A few guys I had been housed with in St. Charles Parish were already there. A few others I recognized from the streets back home. Seeing them didn't make prison easier, but it made the transition smoother. It gave me a starting point. Familiarity matters in unfamiliar environments.

"Prison is still prison, but knowing a few faces makes it less foreign."

Finding My Circle

Not long after settling in, I ran into someone I had grown up with. Seeing him there hit me in a different way. It reminded me how small our world really was. We reconnected quickly. In that environment, shared history creates instant trust. We understood each other without over explaining.

We became close.

I watched his back. He watched mine.

In prison, loyalty isn't loud. It's shown in small actions. Sitting together at chow. Walking together across the yard. Making sure no one tests the other unnecessarily. It's not about being aggressive. It's about being aware.

We ate hookups together when we could. In prison, food becomes more than nutrition — it becomes comfort, status, sometimes even currency. When you find someone you trust enough to split meals with, that matters.

Eventually, we started hustling inside the prison by running a small store operation. It wasn't flashy. It wasn't reckless. It was structured. Commissary items. Hygiene products. Snacks. Small markups. Controlled distribution. The same skills that once operated in the streets adapted to a confined environment.

"You can take the hustler out of the streets, but the hustle finds new walls."

But this time, it felt different.

There was no illusion about long-term gain. There was no fantasy about empire-building. It was survival. It was structure. It was about making time move faster and keeping the mind sharp.

Accepting the Time

As weeks turned into months, I began to accept the reality of my sentence. Eighty-seven months translated into years I couldn't get back. Years my daughter would grow. Years my mom would age. Years that would either shape me or break me.

I chose to let it shape me.

I had already seen what bitterness does to men inside. I had seen what denial does. I had seen how some men live in prison physically but refuse to grow mentally. I didn't want to be that.

"If I had to do the time, the time wasn't going to do me."

Walking into Beaumont wasn't the end of my story.

It was the beginning of the chapter where I had no more excuses.

No more illusions.

No more room to pretend I didn't see the cycle clearly.

And for the first time in a long time, I wasn't thinking about money.

I was thinking about becoming something different than the pattern I came from, but that was easier said than done.

Prison has a rhythm to it. Even in a place built on confinement, there's a flow to the day. You learn when to move, when to sit, when to talk, and when to stay quiet. That afternoon, me and my homie were in the TV room watching something simple, just trying to pass time like everybody else. In prison, television isn't just entertainment — it's distraction. It gives your mind something to hold onto besides walls and time.

Everything felt normal at first.

But in prison, normal can change in seconds.

I noticed the shift before anything was said. Energy changes before words do. A guy approached with tension already in his shoulders. His walk wasn't casual. It was intentional. He wasn't alone either. A few of his homies from up north lingered nearby, pretending not to be involved but clearly positioned.

He started talking aggressively, trying to provoke a reaction. His tone wasn't about resolution. It was about dominance. My homie stayed calm, but tension was building fast. I could feel it tightening in the room. Other inmates were watching without watching. That's how it goes. Everyone senses it, but nobody wants to be the first to move.

Then something small happened — a shove, a word crossed the wrong way — and everything exploded.

It wasn't gradual.

It wasn't controlled.

It erupted.

Once the first swing was thrown, there was no pulling it back. I had my lock in my hand ready for action. The first guy that came my way got knocked out out cold. What could have been a contained situation instantly turned into a full-on gang fight. Bodies collided. Chairs scraped across the floor. The sound of fists landing mixed with shouting. People rushed in from different angles.

Blood appeared faster than I expected.

When multiple men jump into one conflict, it becomes chaos. There's no technique. There's no clean exchange. It's survival. I remember trying to stay upright while blows came from more than one direction. My focus narrowed. My breathing shortened. The room blurred.

Aftermath

Eventually, officers stormed in. Sirens. Orders. Pepper spray in the air. Bodies separating. Men pulled apart and thrown to the ground. The chaos that had consumed the room was suddenly replaced with controlled force.

I was breathing hard, trying to assess whether I was injured because I seen blood on my shirt. But I was good.

My homie was still standing. That was the first relief I felt. We locked eyes briefly — no words needed.

We had survived.

But it had been close.

Very close.

Chapter 17 — Echoes In My Head

When the Walls Start Talking

Prison has a way of getting into your head. Not loud at first. Not dramatic. It creeps in quietly. Out there, life moves fast — money, noise, people always around you, phones ringing, engines running. In here, everything slows down. The doors slam slower. The days drag longer. The nights feel endless. You start hearing your own thoughts louder than anything else.

And when your thoughts are the loudest thing in the room, you can't run from them.

You think about it all. The good times that felt unstoppable. The bad decisions you justified in the moment. The people you lost along the journey — funerals you missed, relationships that fell apart, friends who either folded under pressure or folded on you. And then you think about the ones who are still alive… but somehow you lost them too.

Because prison doesn't just separate you physically. It slowly separates you emotionally.

At first, the phone calls come regularly. People answer with energy. *"We got you. Hold your head."* But as months turn into years, those same calls get shorter. Conversations get dry. The excitement fades. People start living their lives without including you in them. Visits that used to feel automatic become rare. Commissary money that used to come steady starts coming "when I can." You begin to understand something nobody prepares you for — the world adjusts to your absence.

And you're left sitting in a cell adjusting to theirs.

When it got too heavy, when my mind started racing at night and the walls felt like they were closing in, the only two people I could truly count on were my mom and my sister. They didn't always have much, but they had consistency. And consistency in prison feels like oxygen. Just hearing my mom's voice could calm a storm inside me. Just knowing my sister picked up the phone reminded me I wasn't completely erased.

But even with that support… there were nights I felt alone in a way I never felt on the streets.

Grieving Behind Walls

About four months after I got locked up in 2009, I got news that hit different.

My nephew died.

I was already trying to process being in federal prison. Already adjusting to the routine. Already feeling the distance from my daughter. And then that call came.

When you're locked up, bad news doesn't come gently. It doesn't come with comfort. It comes quick. Cold. Clinical.

And then you're left alone with it.

My nephew wasn't just family, he was my dawg "Wild Bill" — we all grew up in the same house together. Tight-knit. Always around each other. Holidays. Cookouts. Running through the same houses, the same streets. He wasn't a distant relative you only saw once a year.

He was part of us.

And just like that, he was gone.

The hardest part wasn't just the loss.

It was being stuck.

Not being able to attend the funeral.
Not being able to hug my family.
Not being able to sit with my mom.
Not being able to grieve properly.

I had to mourn inside a prison.

There's no privacy in prison grief. You don't get space to fall apart. You still have count time. Still have chow. Still have movement. Life keeps moving around you like nothing happened, while your world feels like it just cracked again.

I remember sitting on my bunk that night staring at the wall, thinking, *"How much more can we take?"*

My family was already hurting.
I was already gone.
And now this.

We were losing pieces of ourselves while being separated from each other.

It made the sentence heavier.

Because prison already takes your freedom.
But loss takes your peace.

And when you can't be present for your family during tragedy, it creates a different kind of guilt. A helplessness that sits deep.

That was another layer of trauma.

Another layer of pain.

Another reminder that life doesn't pause just because you're locked up.

Mail Call

Mail call was sacred. It might sound small to someone free, but inside those walls, a letter can carry more weight than money, more weight than reputation. Your name getting called meant you still mattered to someone on the outside.

That day, when they called my name, I tried to stay composed. In prison, you don't show too much emotion. You don't let people read you. But inside, I felt something shift. I walked back to my cell steady, but my heart was beating fast.

I sat down on the edge of my bunk and stared at the envelope for a moment before opening it. I recognized the handwriting. It was from my daughter.

My hands felt heavier than usual.

When I opened it, a few pictures slid out onto my lap. There she was — smiling, growing, changing. Bigger than the last time I saw her. Taller. More mature in her face. Time had moved forward for her… while I was stuck in place.

I studied every photo like I was trying to pause time. I traced the edges of her face with my eyes. I imagined her voice. I imagined what she sounded like now. I wondered if she still needed me the same way. I wondered if she asked about me when I wasn't there.

Then I read her letter.

Simple words. Pure words. Words only a child could write. Telling me about school. About friends. About things that felt so normal — and so far away from my reality. Somewhere between the second and third paragraph, my vision blurred. A tear dropped before I could stop it.

In prison, you try to stay solid. You harden yourself because vulnerability can be dangerous. But that letter cracked something open in me that I didn't even know was still soft.

And OG saw it.

OG's Words

OG had been my cellmate for a while. We weren't the type to sit around talking all day. Prison doesn't work like that. You coexist. You respect space. But OG was different. He moved with a calmness that only comes from someone who's already accepted their reality.

He didn't talk much, but when he did, it meant something.

He watched me sitting there on that bunk, pictures in my hand, tear rolling down my face. He didn't laugh. He didn't look away. He just let the silence sit for a minute.

Then he said, "Nephew… you still got a chance."

I looked up at him, trying to pull myself together.

He continued, voice steady, not loud, not emotional — just real. "You still got a chance to go home and be with your family. Don't waste it."

I didn't say anything.

He leaned back against the wall and added, "I'm here for life. I'll never walk out them gates. I'll never see my kids outside these walls again. The last time I hugged my son, he was your daughter's age. He grown now. I missed it all."

That hit me in a place deeper than fear ever could.

It wasn't a threat.
It wasn't a scare tactic.
It was truth.

A man who had nothing left to gain… telling me I still had everything to lose.

Then he said something that stayed with me forever:

"Don't let this place raise you. Let it teach you."

The Promise

That night, after lights out, I couldn't sleep. I kept replaying his words in my head. *You still got a chance*. Those five words felt heavier than my sentence.

For the first time since being locked up, I stopped thinking about surviving prison and started thinking about surviving life after prison. I realized something — prison can either turn you bitter or it can turn you better. But it won't let you stay the same.

Sitting there on that metal bunk, holding my daughter's pictures against my chest, I made a quiet promise to myself.

I was going home.

And when I did, I wasn't coming back.

I didn't know what I was going to do. I didn't know how I was going to rebuild. I didn't know what doors would even open for a convicted felon. But I knew one thing for sure — I wasn't going to let OG's reality become mine.

I wasn't going to let my daughter grow up visiting me through glass.
I wasn't going to let my mother grow old watching me in a jumpsuit.
I wasn't going to let my name end inside those walls.

That was the night something changed in me.

Not loudly.
Not dramatically.

But permanently.

Becoming a Different Man

After that conversation with OG, something inside me shifted for real. It wasn't loud. I didn't wake up the next morning a brand-new person. But my daily actions started changing. And in prison, your daily actions are everything.

Instead of just counting days, I started making the days count.

I began reading more — not just to pass time, but to understand life. Books on mindset. Books on business. Books on people who came from nothing and built something. Every page felt like I was sharpening something inside myself that had been dull for years. I wasn't just feeding my mind; I was rebuilding it.

I started working out with more purpose too. Not just lifting weights to look strong, but to discipline myself. Every rep became symbolic. Every drop of sweat felt like I was sweating out the old version of me. I told myself, ***"If I can control my body, I can control my decisions."***

And slowly, I was getting myself back together.

Mentor Behind the Walls

Some of the younger guys, I was still young myself, would ask me questions. At first it was small stuff — workout routines, how to move smart in the unit, how to avoid trouble. But then it became deeper. They'd talk about their cases. Their regrets. Their fears.

I saw myself in them.

So I started mentoring them. Not in a loud way. Not trying to be the prison preacher. Just real conversations. I'd tell them, ***"Don't let one mistake turn into a lifetime of them."*** I'd remind them that the streets don't love you back. That loyalty in the free world is temporary, but consequences are permanent.

Even some of the older guys, the ones who felt like it was too late, I'd sit with them too. A few didn't have their GED. Some felt embarrassed about it. I started helping them study. We'd sit at those metal tables going over math problems, reading comprehension, writing paragraphs.

When one of them passed his test, the smile on his face felt bigger than any money I ever made on the outside.

In that moment, I realized something powerful — I felt better helping someone grow than I ever did hustling.

That was new for me.

Earning My Time

My name started being mentioned differently. Not as the guy who came in with a case. Not as the hustler. But as someone who stayed out the way. Someone who read. Someone who helped others.

Officers noticed. In prison, your paperwork follows you, but so does your behavior. I stayed disciplined. No write-ups. No unnecessary drama. I kept hearing OG's voice in my head: ***"Don't let this place raise you. Let it teach you."***

And it was teaching me patience.
It was teaching me humility.
It was teaching me who I really was when everything was stripped away.

Then one day, I heard something I'd been waiting years to hear.

My release date.

The Call to the Gate

It didn't feel real at first. I had imagined that day so many times, but when it actually came, it felt almost quiet. Like the world wasn't celebrating the way my heart was.

I packed my few belongings — papers, books, letters, pictures of my daughter. Everything I owned fit into a small bag. Years of my life reduced to a handful of items.

OG looked at me that morning before I left and said, ***"Go live, nephew. Don't waste it."***

I nodded, but inside I felt something heavy. Excitement mixed with fear. Because prison, as hard as it is, becomes structured. You know the routine. You know the rules. The outside? That's unpredictable.

When they called my name and walked me toward the gate, each step felt like I was walking toward a second chance — but also toward judgment. Toward a world that might not accept me back so easily.

The gate opened.

The air felt different. Fresher. Bigger. Free.

But freedom comes with responsibility.

And as I stepped back into society, I told myself one thing:

I survived prison. Now I have to prove I deserve freedom.

Chapter 18 — Welcome Back

Five Years That Felt Like Fifty

Those were the longest five years of my life.

Not because the calendar said five. But because every single day inside felt stretched. Holidays without family. Birthdays without hugs. Phone calls that ended too fast. Seasons changing through a small window.

When I finally walked out, I thought freedom would feel lighter.

It didn't.

It felt heavy.

Because while I was locked up, the world kept moving. Technology changed. People changed. The streets changed. Even the air felt different. The block didn't look the same. The faces weren't the same. And the few that were… looked at me differently.

I came home thinking I would just plug back into life.

But life had already rewired itself without me.

A Different Kind of Stranger

My daughter had grown.

That was the hardest part.

She wasn't the little girl from the pictures anymore. She had her own personality now. Her own opinions. Her own rhythm. I missed the small things — first days of school, random conversations, moments that can't be recreated. I was home physically, but I had to earn my place back emotionally.

And the truth was, nobody was waiting with a blueprint for me.

No one gave me a few dollars get on my feet.
No one had a savings account set aside.
No one had a plan.

When you come home from prison, people are happy you're free — but that doesn't mean they're prepared to carry you.

I didn't have anything. No real money. No assets. Just determination and a record attached to my name.

So I did what I had to do.

Back Where It Started

I got a job working at a restaurant.

The same restaurant I used to work at years before — back when life felt simpler. Back when I first found out my daughter was about to be born. I can still remember that feeling. The pressure. The fear of not being able to provide. The weight of becoming a father with nothing solid under me.

That was the moment I jumped into selling drugs the first time.

I told myself back then, ***"I need fast money. I don't have time to struggle."***

And that decision cost me five years.

Now here I was again. Same type of job. Same smell of food in the air. Same grind. But this time, I was different.

The uniform felt humbling.

There were moments I'd be cleaning tables or taking orders and my mind would wander. *"How did I end up back here?"* Not in a bitter way. But in a reflective way. Like life had circled me back to the very fork in the road where I made the wrong turn.

Only this time, I chose differently.

Fighting the Old Voice

The temptation was there. Easy money still existed. People still knew my name. Some even reached out like nothing had happened.

"You back? Let's get it."

But OG's voice would echo in my head. ***"You still got a chance."***

I wasn't going back.

Working that restaurant job wasn't glamorous. The pay wasn't great. My pride had to shrink a little. But every honest dollar felt cleaner. Every shift I finished felt like a small victory.

It wasn't about the restaurant.

It was about proving to myself that I could choose discipline over desperation.

Starting From Nothing

Starting over at zero as a grown man hits different. Especially when you've touched money before. Especially when you've lived fast before.

But there's something powerful about building legally what you once tried to rush illegally.

Every late shift.
Every small paycheck.
Every moment I felt overlooked.

It was all shaping me.

Because this time, I wasn't chasing fast money.

I was chasing stability.
I was chasing respect.
I was chasing redemption.

And I didn't know it yet... but this was the foundation for something bigger than I could see at the time.

Wanting More

Working at that restaurant humbled me.

It taught me patience. It taught me discipline. But deep down, I knew I wanted more. Not just more money — more meaning. I didn't survive five years in federal prison just to clock in and clock out for the rest of my life.

One night after a long shift, I sat in my car and asked myself a hard question:

"Is this it?"

And the answer was clear.

No.

I didn't know exactly what the next move was, but I knew it had to involve growth. I needed something that would challenge my mind the same way prison had forced me to challenge my character.

That's when I made a decision that scared me almost as much as prison did.

I enrolled in college.

Stepping Onto Campus

I chose Southern University at New Orleans — **SUNO.**

Walking onto that campus felt surreal. I didn't even know that I could go to college with felony on my record. I was older than a lot of the students. I carried experiences they couldn't see. I carried a record that didn't show on my transcript but followed me everywhere mentally.

At first, I felt out of place.

But I reminded myself: ***"You survived prison. You can survive a classroom."***

When it came time to pick a major, I chose Mathematics. Not because it sounded glamorous. Not because it was easy. But because numbers made sense to me. Math was the closest thing to counting money — and I had always been good at that.

Numbers don't lie.
Equations don't judge.
Formulas reward discipline.

Math felt honest.

A Different Kind of Sentence

What's crazy is this — those four years of college moved faster than the five years I did in federal prison.

In prison, time drags because you're waiting.

In college, time flies because you're building.

Instead of counting days until release, I was counting credits toward graduation. Instead of studying case law and sentencing guidelines, I was studying calculus, statistics, and advanced algebra.

There were nights I barely slept. Mornings I doubted myself. Moments when imposter syndrome crept in and whispered, ***"You don't belong here."***

But every time that voice showed up, I worked harder.

I sat in the front of classrooms.
I asked questions.
I went to tutoring.
I studied like my freedom depended on it.

Because in a way, it did.

Rewriting My Name

The same discipline that helped me survive prison now helped me excel in school.

Professors began to notice. Classmates started asking me for help. The guy who once mentored men in a prison dorm was now tutoring students on campus.

That wasn't accidental.

That was transformation.

Semester after semester, my GPA climbed. I wasn't just passing — I was mastering the material. Math became more than numbers; it became proof that I could rebuild my mind the same way I rebuilt my life.

And then came the moment that felt almost unbelievable.

I finished my degree in less than four years.

Not only did I graduate…

I graduated at the top of my class.

Cum laude.

That phrase hit differently for someone who once wore a federal inmate number.

From prison ID to academic honors.

From a cell block to a graduation stage.

When they called my name, I didn't just hear applause — I heard redemption. I heard OG's voice. I heard my daughter's letter. I heard every doubt I ever had being silenced.

And in that moment, I realized something powerful:

I wasn't just rebuilding my life.

I was rewriting my legacy.

Chapter 19 — College Life With A Twist

Success With a Shadow

While I was rewriting my legacy, something still felt incomplete.

On paper, my life was moving forward. I was in college. My grades were strong. I was rebuilding my name. But every step forward carried a quiet weight.

My brothers were still inside.

Lonk was halfway through a 12-year sentence. Bay Bay was close to coming home. Al was about to be released too. We had all walked similar roads, made similar choices, carried the same hunger at one point. The difference now was timing.

I was the last one to go in.

And the first one to get out.

That reality sat heavy with me.

Sometimes success comes with a strange kind of guilt. I would sit in class solving equations, and my mind would drift to a prison yard somewhere. I'd be walking across campus, free, and picture one of them walking a track in circles.

It didn't feel fair.

But life isn't measured by fairness — it's measured by decisions and timing.

Waiting for the Reunion

I couldn't wait for them to come home.

Not just to celebrate freedom — but to sit somewhere and laugh like we used to. To tell stories about what we survived. To compare scars. To talk about the old days from a new perspective.

I imagined us sitting together one day, not as hustlers, not as inmates — but as men who made it through something.

I kept telling myself, "When they come home, it's going to feel complete."

Because no matter how much I was achieving, there's something about shared history that success can't replace. They understood a version of me that nobody else ever would. The hunger. The ambition. The mistakes. The loyalty.

Brotherhood doesn't dissolve with prison time.

It just waits.

Bay Bay Comes Home

Bay Bay came home first.

It was about a year or two before I graduated. Seeing him outside those walls felt unreal at first. No jumpsuit. No gates. Just regular clothes and real air.

We hugged longer than usual.

There's a silent understanding between men who've done time. You don't have to say much. The hug says it.

He looked at me differently too. I wasn't the same Brennan who left. I was in school. Focused. Structured. Moving different.

He told me, ***"You really doing this college thing for real?"***

I laughed and said, "Yeah… I had to switch the game up."

But inside, it meant more than that. Him seeing me on a different path felt important. Not in a bragging way. But in a leadership way.

If one of us could pivot… maybe all of us could.

Different Directions, Same Roots

Al was about to come home too. Lonk still had time to serve. And every time I thought about him sitting halfway through twelve years, I felt that same quiet pressure.

I was free.

They weren't.

I was building something.

They were still surviving.

That contrast pushed me harder. I didn't want my freedom wasted. I didn't want my degree to just be a personal accomplishment. I wanted it to represent something bigger — proof that our story didn't have to end where it started.

Because we all went in behind the same kind of lifestyle.

But maybe we didn't all have to come out the same way.

Incomplete, But Evolving

Even as I walked toward graduation, even as cum laude got added to my name, part of me was still waiting.

Waiting for the day all of us would be home.
Waiting for the day we could sit in the same room again.
Waiting for the day we could look at each other and say, *"We survived it."*

I realized something during that time though — freedom isn't just physical. It's mental. And while I couldn't open their gates, I could prepare a different blueprint for when they walked through theirs.

Because I was no longer just rewriting my legacy.

I was trying to rewrite ours.

The Call I Wasn't Ready For

Not long after Bay Bay came home, I started noticing the shift. At first it was subtle — old faces popping back up, old corners calling his name, the same rhythm of the streets pulling at him like it never let him leave. We would talk, and I tried not to sound like I was preaching. I'd just say little things like, *"We got another chance now."* But the streets have a grip on you. Especially when that's all you've known. Before I even graduated, before I got the chance to walk across that stage, I got the call that changed everything. Bay Bay had been shot — shot in the head — right there at Orleans Avenue and Claiborne Avenue, the same area he used to hang, the same environment we grew up in, the same place we thought we understood. He didn't make it.

A Stage With a Missing Face

When I heard the news, everything went quiet inside me. We had just hugged not long ago. We had just talked about freedom. We had just imagined sitting together one day, reminiscing about what we survived. And now he was gone. I kept thinking about how close he was to seeing me graduate. How close he was to watching me walk across that stage and hearing my name called. He never got that chance. Never saw the cap and gown. Never got to witness what we were capable of becoming. When graduation day came and they announced that I finished cum laude, my family was proud. My mom. My sister. My daughter. But in my heart, there was a missing face in the crowd. I wasn't just walking for me that day. I was walking for Bay Bay too.

The Weight of Survival

His death hit me harder than prison ever did. I cried, I cried, I cried, The tears came uncontrollable. Prison tests your patience and endurance, but loss tests your soul. I found myself replaying conversations in my head, wondering if I could have said more, done more, pushed harder. *"What if he stayed focused? What if we both left the streets alone sooner?"* But "what if" doesn't bring anyone back. What it does is force you to see the truth. Coming home from prison doesn't mean you've escaped if your mindset stays locked up in the same place. If your environment doesn't change, if your habits don't change, if your circle doesn't change, you're still trapped — just without bars. Bay Bay went back to what felt familiar, and sometimes familiarity is the most dangerous thing in the world. His story didn't get the redemption arc mine did, and that realization put a different kind of fire in me. Now my success wasn't just about proving something to myself. It was about breaking a cycle that had already taken too much from us.

Chapter 20 — Another Celebration, Another Loss

The Last One Standing

I graduated.

I walked across that stage carrying pride, pain, and promise all at once. I had already lost Bay Bay before that moment, and I told myself I had to stay strong. I had to keep building. I had to keep pushing. Not just for me — but for all of us.

Not long after graduation, Al came home.

Seeing him step back into the world felt like hope trying to breathe again. After everything we had been through — prison, funerals, setbacks — I thought maybe this time would be different. Maybe this was our chance to rebuild what had been broken. We talked about the future. We talked about doing better. We talked about not wasting time.

But life doesn't always give you time.

Not long after coming home, Al suffered a stroke.

And just like that… he was gone.

Another brother dead.

From Five to One

My mom had five boys.

Five voices in her house.
Five personalities.
Five futures she prayed over.

Now she was down to one.

I can only imagine the weight she carries. A mother is not supposed to bury her children. She carried us for nine months each, raised us, fed us, fought for us — and now she has to live with empty seats at holidays, empty phone calls, empty spaces where laughter used to live.

When I look at her now, I see strength… but I also see heartbreak she tries not to show.

Losing one child is devastating.
Losing two?

That kind of pain doesn't have language.

Sometimes I sit and think about what it must feel like for her. To watch one son graduate college while grieving two others. Pride and pain existing in the same heartbeat.

I am her only son left.

That reality humbles me every day.

The Weight Lonk Carries

And then there's Lonk.

Still serving his time.

Still waking up behind walls.

Within a 12-year sentence, he lost two brothers. Two funerals he couldn't attend. Two goodbyes he never got to say. Two hugs he'll never feel again.

There's a different kind of torture in that.

Being locked up is one thing.

But being locked up while the world outside is falling apart?

That's another level of helplessness.

I think about him sitting in a cell getting that news. No comfort. No privacy to grieve. Just concrete walls and a thin mattress. Trying to process loss in a place that doesn't allow you to fully break down.

He lost two brothers while doing time.

I lost two brothers while trying to rebuild.

And my mother lost two sons while trying to stay strong for the rest of us.

The Responsibility of the Last One Standing

Sometimes I ask myself why.

Why am I still here?
Why did I make it home?
Why did I graduate?
Why am I the last one standing?

There's a responsibility that comes with surviving.

It's not just about success anymore.
It's about stewardship.

It's about legacy.
It's about making sure their names don't fade into just memories.

I carry them with me everywhere I go.

In every decision.
In every achievement.
In every quiet moment when I sit alone and reflect.

My mom had five boys.

Now she has one.

And I don't take a single day lightly because of that.

Not anymore.

Chapter 21 — The Beginning Of The New Me

From the Streets to the Front of the Classroom

There are transformations… and then there are rebirths.

I didn't just switch careers.

I didn't just "get a job."

I crossed worlds.

I went from selling drugs full-time — living fast, moving in silence, calculating risk every day — to standing in front of a classroom teaching mathematics. From federal inmate to educator. From a prison ID number to "Mr." in front of my name.

Sometimes I still pause and say it out loud to myself:

"How did I get here?"

The same mind that once calculated profit margins on illegal transactions was now solving equations on a whiteboard. The same discipline that once helped me survive federal prison was now helping students pass exams. The same intensity that once kept me alert in the streets was now focused on lesson plans, tutoring sessions, and test prep.

That's not a small change.

That's transformation.

Teaching Was More Than a Job

When I stepped into that classroom for the first time, I wasn't just there to teach math.

I was there to interrupt cycles.

Some of those kids reminded me of myself — restless, distracted, carrying things they didn't talk about. Some came from environments where survival was louder than education. I could see it in their eyes.

And instead of judging them, I understood them.

I'd tell them things like, "Your current situation doesn't decide your final destination."
Or, "You're smarter than you think — you just haven't applied it yet."

I wasn't just teaching equations.

I was teaching discipline.
I was teaching structure.
I was teaching possibility.

Because math, like life, rewards consistency.

Coaching Beyond the Board

It didn't stop in the classroom.

I started coaching too.

Sports had always been in me. Even back when I was watching SportsCenter the morning the feds kicked in my door. That competitive fire never left — it just needed to be redirected.

On the court, on the field, in practice drills — I saw opportunity. Coaching gave me another lane to pour into kids. To teach accountability. To teach teamwork. To teach them how to channel frustration into performance instead of destruction.

I'd tell them, "Energy is energy. It's up to you how you use it."

Some of them didn't even realize they were learning life lessons.

But they were.

And so was I.

Healing While Helping

The truth is, while I was teaching them… they were healing me.

Every student who passed a test.
Every athlete who improved their discipline.
Every kid who said, "Thank you."

It patched a part of me that prison and loss had torn open.

I had lost three brothers.
I had watched my mother bury sons.
I had carried survivor's guilt heavier than any sentence.

But standing in that classroom, hearing "Good morning, Mr." reminded me that my life still had impact.

"Maybe this is why I survived."

Helping them stay focused helped me stay focused. Guiding them away from bad decisions reinforced my own commitment to never go back. Watching them grow reminded me that growth is always possible.

I wasn't just earning a paycheck.

I was earning peace.

Where It All Started Paying Off

This was the moment everything started making sense.

The prison time. The losses. The long nights studying.
The restaurant job. The discipline. The grief.
The graduation.

It all converged into purpose.

I went from selling poison in my community to pouring knowledge into it.

From contributing to destruction…
To building foundations.

From surviving…
To serving a purpose.

And that shift — that complete reversal of direction — is where it all started paying off.

Because success isn't just about money or titles.

It's about alignment.

And for the first time in my life, who I was… matched who I was becoming.

"I didn't just change my career. I changed my legacy."

"You Changed My Life"

It didn't happen at a big ceremony.

There was no spotlight. No applause. No announcement over a loudspeaker.

It happened on an ordinary afternoon after class.

Most of the students had already packed up and left. The room was quieter than usual. Papers were still scattered on a few desks. I was at my table grading assignments when one of my students lingered by the door. He wasn't my top student. In fact, when he first came into my class, he was the one who barely paid attention, always half-checked out, carrying that same restless energy I used to carry.

He walked back toward my desk slowly and said, *"Can I talk to you for a minute?"*

I nodded.

He hesitated at first. Looked down. Took a breath.

Then he said something I'll never forget.

"I was about to quit."

I didn't say anything. I just listened.

He went on to tell me about what was going on at home. About the pressure. About how easy it would be to start making fast money. About friends already pulling him toward the streets. He told me there were days he didn't even see the point in school.

Then he looked up at me and said, "But when you told us you came from nothing and still made it… that hit me."

I felt my chest tighten.

He continued, "You don't talk down to us. You talk like you understand. And when you say we can do better, it don't sound fake. It sounds real."

Then he said the words that stopped time for a second.

"You changed my life."

I had stood in front of classrooms hundreds of times. I had solved complex equations. I had graduated cum laude. I had survived federal prison. But nothing — nothing — hit like that moment.

Because this was different.

This wasn't about grades.
This wasn't about a title.
This wasn't about redemption for me.

This was impact.

I leaned back in my chair, trying to hold it together, and told him, *"I didn't change your life. You decided to."*

But deep down, I understood something powerful.

This was why I survived.

All the years in prison.
All the loss.

All the grief.
All the discipline.
All the studying.
All the rebuilding.

It wasn't just to prove I could change.

It was to show someone else they could too.

As he walked out of that classroom, I sat there for a minute in silence. I thought about Bay Bay. I thought about Al. I thought about my mom. I thought about Lonk sitting in a cell.

And I whispered to myself,

"This is what it was all for."

Chapter 21 — Breaking The Bloodline of Trauma

Full Circle

What started in one classroom turned into something bigger than I ever imagined. I began mentoring kids all over the city — not because I was chasing recognition, but because I understood them. I had lived every version of their struggle. The anger. The silence. The survival mode. The pain you don't know how to explain because nobody ever gave you the language for it. That was me once. So when I sit with them now, I don't see "bad kids." I see trauma. I see fear. I see potential buried under pressure. I tell them, *"You're not broken. You're responding to what you've been through."* And sometimes that sentence alone changes how they see themselves.

As the work grew, so did the attention. I was featured on the front page of the newspaper — something I never could have imagined during the years when my name was only associated with a federal case. I also have a billboard downtown with my face on it, because of the work I put in as a transformed Man. City leaders began recognizing the transformation, not just in me, but in the students I was reaching. They invited me to speak about what I had learned the hard way: kids are more than statistics. More than test scores. More than suspension numbers. I made it clear every time I spoke,

"You can't discipline trauma out of a child. You have to help them process it."

Because what looks like defiance is often pain. What looks like laziness is often hopelessness. What looks like aggression is often survival.

Then something happened that truly brought everything full circle. A documentary was created about my journey called ***Children of Central City.*** Cameras followed the story — the streets, the prison time, the losses, the graduation, the classroom, the mentoring. It wasn't about glorifying the past. It was about showing the transformation. Schools across the city began adopting a trauma-informed approach in their classrooms, and they started the year by playing that documentary. Students would sit and watch my story — the mistakes, the redemption, the rebuilding — and teachers would tell them,

"If Brennan can do it, you can do it too."

Hearing that humbled me in a way success never could. I went from being a cautionary tale to becoming a case study in resilience. From contributing to the cycle to helping break it. From federal inmate to educator, mentor, and example. And every time a group of students watches that film and sees someone who looks like them, talks like them, and came from what they came from, I know the mission is bigger than me.

Because this was never just about my comeback.

It was about creating proof.

Proof that trauma doesn't have to be destiny.
Proof that mistakes don't have to be permanent.
Proof that transformation is real.

And now when those kids look at me, they don't just see a teacher.

They see possibility.

Looking back, I realize something powerful: my past was shaping my future long before I understood it. The instability. The hospital nights.

The streets. The prison cell. The grief of losing my brothers. The discipline of college. The humility of starting over. Every painful chapter was building perspective. Every mistake was sharpening empathy. Every loss was deepening my purpose. What once felt like setbacks were actually setups for impact.

Now, without even realizing it, I'm shaping futures the same way mine was shaped — but with guidance instead of chaos. Some of these kids don't know it yet. They don't know that the conversation we had after class will stay with them for years. They don't know that the discipline they're learning in practice will carry into adulthood. They don't know that being seen and understood in a classroom can change the trajectory of their lives. But it does.

And I'm still here. Still teaching. Still mentoring. Still walking into classrooms across the New Orleans area with the same mission. Still showing up for kids who remind me of who I used to be. This isn't a finished story. It's ongoing. Every school year is another opportunity. Every student is another chance to interrupt a cycle.

I once contributed to the pain in my community.

Now I contribute to the healing.

"And that's the true full circle — not just surviving my past, but using it as a blueprint to build someone else's future."

Gods Blessing

And somewhere in the middle of all this healing, God blessed me with something else — a son. Brennan Jr.

Now I'm mentoring him too. Not just teaching him math. Not just teaching him sports.
But teaching him presence.

I wasn't always there the way I should have been when my daughter was younger. Prison took years I can't get back. And that's something I carry honestly. But growth means accountability. Growth means doing better when you know better.

With my son, I am intentional.

I show up. I listen. I guide. I correct with love. I protect his peace.
I pour into him daily.

Because breaking cycles isn't something you preach.

It's something you practice.

And every time I sit with him, talk with him, mentor him, laugh with him — I'm not just being a father.

I'm rewriting history.

Carrying The Legacy

When I look back over my life, it doesn't feel like one straight line. It feels like chapters carved out of fire. Trauma. Loss. Prison. Death. Redemption. Graduation. Classrooms. Mentoring. Recognition. Every season felt like it could have broken me. Some of them almost did. I lost brothers. I lost my nephew. I lost time. I lost years I can never get back. My mom went from having five boys to one. Lonk sat behind walls grieving two brothers he couldn't bury. I carried survivor's guilt heavier than any prison sentence.

But I also found purpose.

I went from selling drugs to teaching math. From federal inmate to front-page headlines for doing what's right. From contributing to destruction to helping build healing spaces in classrooms across New Orleans. A documentary now plays in schools telling my story, not to glorify my past, but to show what's possible. Kids sit and watch it, and they're told, *"If Brennan can do it, you can too."* And every time I hear that, I'm reminded that my pain wasn't wasted.

My past shaped my future in ways I didn't understand at the time. The hospital nights. The eviction. The funerals. The prison bunk. The mail from my daughter. OG's words. Every hardship was chiseling something inside me. What felt like punishment was preparation. What felt like loss was leadership training. What felt like survival became service.

Now I walk into classrooms and mentoring sessions knowing I'm not just teaching lessons — I'm interrupting cycles. Some of these kids don't even realize their futures are shifting. They don't know the seeds being planted. But one day they will. One day they'll look back and understand that someone saw them before they saw themselves.

And if you're reading this, understand something important:

My life is not some rare miracle story.

My life is just like yours.

I was born into circumstances I didn't choose. I grew up in environments that shaped my thinking before I understood what thinking even was. I made decisions out of survival. I felt trapped. I felt like there was no way out. If you've ever felt that way — like the odds were stacked too high, like the streets were louder than your dreams, like your trauma defined you — then this story is for you.

This is for the ones who were born into chaos.
This is for the ones who lost people too early.
This is for the ones who made mistakes and thought that was the end.
This is for the ones who felt forgotten.

You are not alone.

Your beginning does not dictate your ending.

I am not proud of every chapter of my story.

But I am proud that I didn't let the worst parts define the final page.

I'm still here.
Still teaching.
Still mentoring.
Still healing.
Still carrying the names of the ones we lost.

I was once a product of trauma.

Now I am proof that trauma doesn't get the final word.

And if I can rise from where I started…

Then so can you.

This is for you.

This is for us.

Change your bloodline of trauma!!!

Acknowledgments

This book would not exist without the people who stood with me when the world felt too heavy to carry.

To my **mother**, the foundation of my faith and the heart of my strength. You taught me endurance when the world was unkind, love when life felt cruel, and faith when I didn't believe in myself. Your sacrifices built the man I am today. Every word in this book carries your courage and grace.

To my **brothers who are no longer here, Bay-Bay, Alfred and Anthony** , your names are carved into my spirit. I carry your memory in every breath, every lesson, and every act of love I give to this world. You taught me the cost of survival and the value of time. Losing you changed me, but your strength still lives through me — through every life I touch and every young soul I try to save.

To my **brother Rivers**, who still walks beside me, reminding me of where I come from and why I keep going. You've shown me that real strength isn't loud — it's steady.

To my **sister Jynika**, whose love and laughter brought light to my darkest days. You are the reflection of the hope I once thought I'd lost.

To my **daughter Bre'anna**, my heart in human form — you gave me a reason to change, a reason to rise, and a reason to keep believing that healing is possible. You are my purpose and my peace.

To my **son Brennan Jr**, who carries my name and my hope. You inspire me to be better every day, to lead with patience and purpose, and to show you that legacy isn't what you're given — it's what you build.

And to my **family**, both blood and chosen — every one of you who believed in me, prayed for me, and never stopped calling me "home." Your love became the foundation that held this story together.

This book is not just mine — it's ours.
Because every lesson, every scar, every triumph belongs to the people who never gave up on me.

Thank you for being my roots, my reason, and my reminder that love outlasts pain — and that even in loss, legacy lives on.

About the Author

Greetings, I am **Brennan Jacques**, and I stand before you as a black man who shattered the limitations imposed upon me at birth. Rather than accepting the assigned narrative, I seized the power to redefine myself, becoming the architect of my destiny and a catalyst for change in this world.

As the youngest of six siblings, my journey has been shaped by the profound influence of family. However, the path I tread was not without its trials and tribulations, for I encountered a multitude of challenges during my formative years. In my early years, I found myself caught in the grip of adversity, succumbing to the lure of a dangerous path. Selling drugs became a means of survival, leading me down a destructive road that eventually landed me in prison. However, this setback served as a turning point in my life—a wake-up call that propelled me towards a path of redemption and resilience.

Determined to break free from the chains that bound me, I committed myself to personal growth and transformation. While incarcerated, I immersed myself in self-education, devouring books and expanding my knowledge in various subjects. This thirst for knowledge became the catalyst for my remarkable journey of empowerment.

Upon my release, I embraced education as my passport to a brighter future. With unwavering dedication and relentless pursuit of excellence, I embarked on an educational journey that culminated in graduating from college at the top of my class. This achievement not only marked a milestone in my own life but also ignited a fervent desire to empower others through education.

Recognizing the transformative power of mentorship and coaching, I committed myself to becoming a guiding light for those in my community. I emerged as a compassionate teacher, mentor, and coach, tirelessly investing my time and energy in nurturing the potential of young minds. My genuine passion for making a difference in the lives of others became the cornerstone of my life's mission.

As an astute entrepreneur, I channeled my drive and resourcefulness into creating opportunities for myself and my community. I understood that financial empowerment was vital in breaking the cycle of generational obstacles. With remarkable tenacity, I launched successful ventures, providing employment opportunities and economic stability for those around me.

My role as a devoted father to two wonderful children further solidified my commitment to rewriting the narrative of my family's future. I vowed that the ceiling of my own life

would serve as the floor for my children, instilling in them the belief that dreams have no limits.

Driven by an unyielding desire to uplift my community, I have dedicated my life to serving others. I spearhead initiatives to raise funds and organize impactful events that inspire and empower individuals to overcome their obstacles. My unwavering dedication and indomitable spirit have transformed countless lives and created a ripple effect of positive change.

My story was later featured in the acclaimed documentary ***Children of Central City***, which explored the hidden effects of trauma on young men growing up in violent neighborhoods.

In me, you find a remarkable example of resilience, determination, and unwavering belief in the human potential. I stand as a testament to the fact that, no matter the circumstances, one can rise above and transform adversity into triumph. My unwavering commitment to serving others and creating a brighter future for my community, hopefully will inspire us all to reach for greatness, overcome obstacles, and embrace the power of education, mentorship, and entrepreneurship.

Index

Made in the USA
Coppell, TX
20 March 2026

73779717R00095